The Battle for Your Mind

Understanding the Sanctified Personality

THE STEPPING-STONE SERIES

SCRIPTURAL GUIDES TO A BETTER LIFE

★—to Life in the Spirit
The Battle for Your Mind

—to Joy in the Home and Family
Keeping Love in the Family

—to a Winning Life
How Attitudes Make or Break Your Life

The Battle for Your Mind

Understanding the Sanctified Personality

by
Leslie Parrott

BHH

Beacon Hill Press of Kansas City
Kansas City, Missouri

Permission to quote from the following copyrighted versions is acknowledged with appreciation:

The Holy Bible, New International Version (NIV), copyright © 1973, 1978, 1984 by the International Bible Society.

The Living Bible (TLB), © 1971 by Tyndale House Publishers, Wheaton, Ill.

10 9 8 7 6 5 4 3 2

Contents

III
The Fulfilled Life and
the Transformed Mind

Foreword

What did Jesus mean when He told His followers in the Sermon on the Mount that they were to be perfect as their Father in heaven is perfect? This question has intrigued commentators, theologians, and humble believers ever since Jesus uttered it. Some in the church's history have insisted that He was pointing to a state unattainable in this life but one to which the believer should perpetually aspire. Others have seen in this a reference to a level of Christian living and devotion that some noble souls have reached. The text though was never a point of major disagreement until John Wesley.

John Wesley took this text seriously. Linking it with numerous other references to perfection, he made it a major item on the theological agenda. To his own discomfort at times and to the amusement and scorn of his theological enemies he concluded that the sincere believer not only could but should attain to this life of "qualified perfection."

The qualifications were expressed in phrases like Christian perfection and perfection of love. But regardless of the qualifications his position was seen and labeled as perfectionism: When he made it the climax of the order of salvation for the believer in this life, he made sure by that action that this text would be a crux passage for his theological heirs. It meant also that the whole subject of Christian perfection would be part of the theological discussion and spiritual aspiration of the church thenceforth.

Is it possible for Jesus' desire for the believer to be perfected realizable in this life? If so, can that state be maintained? Can we know what constitutes that perfection so that we can know whether we have attained? If it can be attained, what is the process necessary to reach it, and how can the state be maintained? These are the questions that this volume addresses.

The author brings a rich background to his subject. A pastor, evangelist, educator, and administrator, Dr. Leslie Parrott uses all of his experience, insights, and expertise to explicate his subject. The work is practical.

The author's intent is not a systematic treatment for the theologian, but one useful for the ordinary believer. His desire also is to be biblical. The reader will find when he has finished the work that he has been forced to look at a surprising number of the most important passages in the Bible that deal with personal holiness. The work is pastoral. Dr. Parrott's pastoral experience and concern show through. Laymen and pastors alike will find this volume interesting, stimulating, and instructive. My own wish for it is a broad reading especially in our own Wesleyan circles. It should help many to a better understanding and consequently to a greater freedom in Christ.

DENNIS F. KINLAW

Introduction

For years I struggled with the difference between *carnal* nature and *human* nature. I read books and heard sermons that described human nature, which was called carnal. This made sensitive people feel guilty. Then I read books, particularly in psychology, sociology, and anthropology, that described carnal behavior, which was called human. Sin was changed to sickness and guilt to anxiety. The focus was shifted from the sinful self to the maladjusted environment. And in the end either distortion of carnal nature or human nature left a wake of confusion in its path toward the ultimate frustrations of personalities dominated by guilt and anxiety.

This confusion over the difference between human nature and carnal nature has crept into the church, and distortions of both have been proclaimed. These studies, which are based on stepping-stones toward a fulfilled life, are not exhaustive, but they lead in the right direction. They are not clinical, but they are pastoral. They are not technical, but they are biblical.

These stepping-stones have been chosen as devotional guides and not as psychological answers. However, every effort has been made to be true to both the scriptural insights and to current studies in human understanding.

LESLIE PARROTT

I

HUMAN NATURE, CARNAL NATURE, AND PERFECTION

Chapter *1*

The Spirit like a River

Scriptural Stepping-stones

And Jesus commanded . . .

> (the disciples) *that they should not depart from Jerusalem,*

but wait for the promise . . .

> *of the Father, which, . . . ye have heard of me. For John truly baptized with water; but ye shall be baptized with the Holy Ghost not many days hence.*

Acts 1:4-5

*   *   *

The day of Pentecost . . .

> *was fully come, they were all with one accord in one place. And suddenly there came a sound from heaven as of a rushing mighty wind, and it filled all the house where they were sitting. And there appeared unto them cloven tongues like as of fire, and it sat upon each of them. And they were all filled with the Holy Ghost, and began to speak with other tongues, as the Spirit gave them utterance.*

Acts 2:1-4

*   *   *

Behold their threatenings: . . .

> *and grant unto thy servants, that with all boldness they may speak thy word . . . And when they had prayed, the place*

13

was shaken where they were assembled together; and they were all filled with the Holy Ghost, and they spake the word of God with boldness.

Acts 4:29, 31

From the first page to the last the Bible is uniquely the Book of the Holy Spirit. In the first paragraph of Genesis the scripture says, "The Spirit ... moved upon the face of the waters" (v. 2). And the Holy Spirit is mentioned the last time on the final page of the Book of Revelation: "The Spirit and the bride say, Come. ... take the water of life freely" (22:17). And from the first mention of the Holy Spirit in Genesis to the last reference in Revelation, there is a river like a great flow of spiritual lava winding its way through the entire Bible with the power to work the purposes of God in creating, cleansing, and empowering. The river is wide in some places and narrow in others, and sometimes it goes underground; but it is always there, revealing the work of the Holy Spirit.

But within the Bible there is another book even more uniquely the Book of the Holy Spirit. The Acts of the Apostles is a book within a book that gives us a narrative of the Holy Spirit's work more fully than any other of the 66 books.

The Book of Acts opens with a command and a promise: Jesus *"commanded* [the disciples] that they should not depart from Jerusalem, but wait for the *promise* of the Father, which ... ye have heard of me." Then Jesus explains what the *promise* is: "John truly baptized with water; but ye shall be baptized with the Holy Spirit not many days hence" (1:4-5). And following this command and the promise from our risen Lord, the *Book of Acts tells us how the command was obeyed and*

14

how the promise was fulfilled. Six times in the Book of Acts the Holy Spirit is poured out on believers in a very special kind of spiritual experience.

Upper Room

The second chapter of Acts is a report on the coming of the Holy Spirit on the Day of Pentecost: "And when the day of Pentecost was fully come, they were all with one accord in one place" (v. 1).

And let me stop here long enough to say there is no coming of the Holy Spirit until there is first a spirit of unity among the people. I have heard people say their congregation needs an outpouring of the Holy Spirit that would bring their church together. No, it doesn't work that way. We all come to one accord, and *then* the Holy Spirit comes. We don't have to agree on everything to be of one accord. A chord on the piano may contain four or even five different notes, but they all harmonize together. All we have to do to achieve unity is make a decision to live together happily, in peace and accord. Unity is in the mind, not the circumstances. Nothing short of harmonious accord can open the way for the coming of the Holy Spirit in a congregation.

And even more important, the people were of one accord *in one place.* I need to keep myself reminded that some places are more accessible to the work of the Holy Spirit than others. I am glad for a church with great music, great preaching, and great organization staffed by impressive leaders. But most of all, give me a church that is an easy place for the Holy Spirit to come. I like a college with a beautiful campus, a faculty with high academic standards, and a football team with a winning season. I like academic lectures, fine arts concerts, and life on campus. But most of all, give me a college where it is easy for the Holy Spirit to be poured out in chapel convocations with the faculty and students. The command of Jesus was for the disciples to tarry in Jerusalem. This was to give them time to come to one accord in the right place.

"And suddenly" something very unusual happened. The outpouring of the Holy Spirit is an instantaneous experience followed by lifelong growth and development. But the coming was sudden, focused on a point in time. What they *heard* could best be described as the sound of a strong wind. And what they *saw* could best be described as looking like fire with divided flames that settled down on the heads of the people. It was not a wind and not 120 individual fires, but it sounded like wind and it looked like fire.

Then in Luke's narrative we come to that marvelous phrase that is often used in Acts: *"And they were all filled with the Holy Ghost."* It is true that everyone is going to be filled with something. Some are filled with the spirit of bitterness, some with the spirit of competition, or criticism, or selfishness. It is wonderful to be filled with the Holy Spirit because any other spirit is self-defeating and counterproductive.

Jerusalem

In the fourth chapter of Acts the 120 who were filled with the Holy Spirit were filled again along with many others who had been converted during the Jerusalem revival.

Peter and John went up to the Temple at the hour of prayer (Acts 3:1). And let's stop here long enough to say that being filled with the Spirit will help you go to church at the regular time even when you feel like the people in charge are not on your side. When Peter and John went up to the Temple at the regular hour of prayer, it was not because they felt accepted. The clergy in charge and the lay leaders on the Sanhedrin were the men responsible for the crucifixion of Jesus and would have eliminated Peter and John also if they could have. Peter and John must have known this, yet they went to church anyhow because the Holy Spirit gave them the motivation to do what was right.

And, while doing what was right, Peter and John became the agents of the Holy Spirit in the healing of the lame man at the Gate Beautiful (Acts 3:2-8). This public healing wrought havoc in the bureaucracy because the people inside the Temple came outside onto Solomon's porch to see these men who had done this healing. And Peter, who could not pass up the opportunity, preached a sermon to these curious spectators. The healing was bad enough, but the sermon brought down the wrath of the priests, who ordered Peter and John arrested and jailed. The next day, after a bad night, they were brought in before the officialdom to be judged and told forthrightly not to teach or preach anymore in the name of the Lord Jesus. When they let Peter and John go, these shaken leaders of the new believers went back to their own company.

Peter and John had been filled with the Holy Spirit on the Sunday of Pentecost (Acts 4:13-18). And the scripture says Peter was "filled with the Holy Spirit" (v. 8, NIV) when he spoke to the rulers and elders. But he was still frightened. There is not one of us who does not have some persons or some situations that threaten to the point of paralyzing fear. When this kind of fear hits us we usually choose one of two

17

options: We yell louder or we run faster. But there is a third option, and that is a new touch of the Holy Spirit to help us keep cool, help us hold steady, and help us keep on doing what God has appointed us to do.

Peter and John and the company of their friends began to pray a prayer that was just as open and honest as any prayer in the Bible. "And now, Lord, *behold their threatenings:* and grant unto thy servants, that with all boldness they may speak thy word . . . And when they had prayed, the place was shaken where they were assembled together." Then comes that wonderful phrase characteristic of the Book of Acts, *"And they were all filled with the Holy Ghost"* (4:29, 31).

Samaria

In the eighth chapter of Acts, Philip went up to Samaria, a territory forbidden to any self-respecting Jew. There is not time or need for me to characterize Samaria except to say, If you could have a revival in Samaria, you could have a revival anywhere. But in Samaria, the forbidden ghetto between Jerusalem and Nazareth, they had a great revival. It was the kind of revival that would have made national news. I am sure there would have been a news story on the magician, Simon, who tried to buy the kind of power that produced the results he saw in that revival.

But there is a second chapter to the Samaritan story: "Now when the apostles which were at Jerusalem heard that Samaria had received the word of God, they sent unto them Peter and John: who, when they were come down, prayed for them, that they *might receive the Holy Ghost: (for as yet he*

18

was fallen upon none of them: only they were baptized in the name of the Lord Jesus)" (8:14-16).

And then, Dr. Luke gives us another statement on the coming of the Holy Spirit: *"Then laid they their hands on them, and they received the Holy Ghost"* (v. 17). They were converted in a spirit of great revival, and subsequently they were filled with the Holy Spirit.

Damascus

In the ninth chapter of Acts, Saul of Tarsus was converted in a dramatic experience on the road to Damascus when a great light blinded him, and he dropped to his knees, crying, "Lord, what wilt thou have me to do?" (v. 6). The Lord then led Saul into Damascus to the home of a Christian who lived on the street called Straight. (Incidentally, the street called Straight is not called Straight because it is straight, but because it is not as crooked as the other streets in Damascus.) Here Paul waited in blindness and without food or water for three days until a Christian pastor named Ananias came to see him. His voice must have sounded like the waters of heaven to the thirsting soul of Saul, for Ananias came through the door, calling him a brother. *"Brother Saul,* the Lord, even Jesus, that appeared unto thee in the way as thou camest, hath sent me, that thou mightest *receive thy sight,* and *be filled with the Holy Ghost"* (v. 17).

And there is that wonderful phrase again, *"Filled with the Holy Spirit"* (NIV). Saul's conversion ignited a wall of fire against him. But he outmaneuvered his adversaries with a dramatic escape over the wall in a basket. Scholars tell us Saul withdrew at this point into the desert of Arabia where he worked as a tentmaker to support himself for two years while he spent long days in contemplation. He thought through the meaning of the cross of Christ, His resurrection, and the coming of the Holy Spirit. This interpretation of the gospel is what Paul later drafted into his theological letters to the Romans and the Galatians.

Caesarea

The 10th chapter of Acts contains the marvelous story of Cornelius. The scripture says, "There was a certain man in Caesarea called Cornelius, a centurion of the band called the Italian band, a *devout man,* and *one that feared God with all his house, which gave much alms* to the people, and prayed to God alway. He saw in a vision evidently about the ninth hour of the day an angel of God coming in to him, and saying unto him, Cornelius. And when he looked on him, he was afraid, and said, What is it, Lord? And he said unto him, *Thy prayers and thine alms are come up for a memorial before God"* (vv. 1-4).

Then the story reaches its climax in verse 44 when the scripture says, "While Peter yet spake these words, *the Holy Ghost fell on all them that heard the word."* Cornelius, the man of the sterling spiritual qualities, was unfulfilled until the Holy Spirit fell on him and his family.

Ephesus

The sixth and final outpouring of the Holy Spirit in Acts is recorded in the 19th chapter. When Paul visited the city of

Ephesus he met with the church board and heard an excellent report on the quality and the prospects of their church. But when they finished with all their reporting, Paul stopped the meeting cold when he asked them a disconcerting question, "Have ye received the Holy Ghost *since* ye believed?" (v. 2).

They looked at each other with open, honest faces of confusion. Finally one of the men must have said what the others were thinking. "We have not so much as heard whether there be any Holy Ghost."

In response to their openness and their lack of understanding about the Holy Spirit, Paul did three things: (1) He taught them about the Holy Spirit. (2) He preached to them about the Holy Spirit. And (3) He prayed for them. Then the scripture says, "And when Paul had laid his hands on them, *the Holy Ghost came on them"* (v. 6), and the greatest revival in the entire New Testament, outside of the Day of Pentecost, came when one dozen men at the church in Ephesus were filled with the power of the Holy Spirit.

A concluding word: The Book of Acts is not only a book of history covering the early Christian era but also the narrative account of the Spirit's therapy in changing the personalities of those first-generation Christians. Peter and Paul are probably the most dramatic examples of the power of the Holy Spirit to effect change in believers who were filled with His presence. But the Spirit was the Presence who fulfilled all believers.

Chapter 2

The Spirit Is a Person

Scriptural Stepping-stones

Wait for the promise . . .

> *And, being assembled together with them, commanded them that they should not depart from Jerusalem, but wait for the promise of the Father, which, saith he, ye have heard of me.*
>
> Acts 1:4

> *But ye shall receive power, after that the Holy Ghost is come upon you: and ye shall be witnesses unto me both in Jerusalem, and in all Judaea, and in Samaria, and unto the uttermost part of the earth.*
>
> Acts 1:8

* * *

Seven men of honest report . . .

> *Wherefore, brethren, look ye out among you seven men of honest report, full of the Holy Ghost and wisdom, whom we may appoint over this business.*
>
> Acts 6:3

> *But we will give ourselves continually to prayer, and to the ministry of the word.*
>
> Acts 6:4

And the word of God increased; and the number of the disciples multiplied in Jerusalem greatly; and a great company of the priests were obedient to the faith.

Acts 6:7

✳   ✳   ✳

Only they were baptized . . .

Now when the apostles which were at Jerusalem heard that Samaria had received the word of God, they sent unto them Peter and John: who, when they were come down, prayed for them, that they might receive the Holy Ghost: (For as yet he was fallen upon none of them: only they were baptized in the name of the Lord Jesus.) Then laid they their hands on them, and they received the Holy Ghost.

Acts 8:14-17

✳   ✳   ✳

Brother Saul . . .

the Lord, even Jesus, that appeared unto thee in the way as thou camest, hath sent me, that thou mightest receive thy sight, and be filled with the Holy Ghost.

Acts 9:17

✳   ✳   ✳

A devout man . . .

There was a certain man in Caesarea called Cornelius, a centurion of the band called the Italian band, a devout man, and one that feared God with all his house, which gave much alms to the people, and prayed to God alway. . . . And he said unto him, Thy prayers and thine alms are come up for a memorial before God.

Acts 10:1-2, 4b

* * *

Since ye believed . . .

> *[Paul] said unto them, Have ye received the Holy Ghost since ye believed? And they said unto him, We have not so much as heard whether there be any Holy Ghost. . . . And when Paul had laid his hands upon them, the Holy Ghost came on them; and they spake with tongues, and prophesied.*
>
> Acts 19:2, 6

* * *

Separate me Barnabas and Saul . . .

> *for the work whereunto I have called them. . . . So they, being sent forth by the Holy Ghost, . . .*
>
> Acts 13:2b, 4a

* * *

Forbidden by the Holy Spirit . . .

> *Now when they had gone throughout Phrygia and the region of Galatia, and were forbidden of the Holy Ghost to preach the word in Asia, after they were come to Mysia, they assayed to go into Bithynia: but the Spirit suffered them not.*
>
> Acts 16:6-7
>
> *There stood a man of Macedonia, and prayed him, saying, Come over into Macedonia, and help us.*
>
> Acts 16:9b

In the Book of Acts (1) There is the *command*, "Do not leave Jerusalem" (1:4, NIV). (2) There is the *promise*, "Ye shall receive power, after that the Holy Ghost is come upon you."

And (3) There is the *fulfillment* of the promise no less than six times. The Holy Spirit was poured out twice on the disciples and their converts in Jerusalem, and then successively on believers in Samaria, Damascus, Caesarea, and in Ephesus. Besides these six outpourings, the Holy Spirit is the reference point for almost everything else in the Book of Acts. In chapter 6 the Jerusalem church is instructed to choose a church board of Spirit-filled men (vv. 1-8). In chapter 13 the Holy Spirit instructed the church in Antioch to separate out Paul and Barnabas for the special work to which they had been called (v. 2), and Paul and Barnabas became Christ's first full-time missionaries. In chapter 16, Paul and Silas were forbidden by the Holy Spirit to preach in Asia, and instead they responded to the call from Macedonia that brought the gospel from Asia to the continent of Europe (vv. 6-9). Western civilization became Christian in its values and its theology because the Holy Spirit led Paul to hear the voice calling from Macedonia. And on and on the river of the Spirit flows through 28 wonderful chapters. The Book of Acts is the narrative report on the acts of the Holy Spirit in the Early Church.

But here is the question I have for you: Taken as a whole—all 28 chapters—what is today's message for you and me in the Book of Acts? The Holy Spirit has said more things to us in Acts than I can ever comprehend. But it does seem to me, as a point of beginning, the command and the promise of Jesus in Acts say three very important things to us today.

A Person and Not a Theology

First, the Book of Acts makes it clear that the Holy Spirit is a person and not a theology. The Holy Spirit is not a thing.

He is not an it. He is not a blessing and not even an experience. The Holy Spirit is a person as God is a person or as our risen Lord is a person. And because He is a person, we have a relationship with Him. We can grieve Him, reject Him, or deny Him. Or we can love Him, obey Him, and live in fellowship with Him. But whatever we do, the Holy Spirit is a person and not a theology.

In my younger years I saw the Holy Spirit mostly as a theology. Very early I learned the five cardinal elements in the doctrine of sanctification through the Holy Spirit. In fact, my theology professor, Dr. S. S. White, wrote a book called *The Five Cardinal Elements in Sanctification.* They are (1) the second definite work of grace, (2) wrought instantaneously by the faith of the believer. (3) Sanctification cleanses or eradicates the heart of inbred sin. (4) The experience is attainable in this life. And (5) Sanctification and the baptism with the Holy Spirit are simultaneous though different experiences of His work. These five cardinal elements are still standard, and I believe them all.

However, I tended to think of the Holy Spirit almost exclusively in these theological concepts. This kind of philosophical approach to the Holy Spirit opened up great opportunity for arguments and debates. As students, we talked about the thief on the cross and debated whether it was possible for him to have had a second definite work of grace subsequent to regeneration when he believed on Christ in the last moments of his life. And still Jesus said, "To day shalt thou be with me in paradise" (Luke 23:43). We had unending arguments on eradication and the inconsistencies we saw in the lives of holiness people, even church leaders. We had great confusion and never settled the question on the difference between human nature and carnal nature. Our approach to the doctrine of the Holy Spirit and entire sanctification was not very helpful in cleaning up our confusion, but it did generate heated discussions.

Then during my first year out of college, I was called to preach in a youth camp on the Hudson River above New York City. Since the counselors were mostly young pastors, we soon had a discussion going on the theology of holiness. One afternoon we were gathered near the tabernacle around a big tree stump, discussing our favorite theological questions. I noticed an old pastor at an uninvolved distance listening but not saying anything. When we had finally worn ourselves down, he came over to have a word. He had been pastor of the same church on Long Island for more than 25 years. He was a godly man with great spiritual wisdom. He said, "If you young men will quit debating the theology of holiness and just pray for the Holy Spirit to come, when He comes He will do whatever needs to be done." I never got away from the last phrase: "When *He* comes *He* will do whatever needs to be done."

I went back to the Book of Acts and began to study it again. And little by little I began to understand the confirming evidence that the Holy Spirit is a person and not a theology. He is the adorable Third Person of the Trinity with whom we may have a fulfilled relationship. He is the strength of our lives for coping with whatever the day affords.

A Presence and Not a Quick Fix

Second, I have learned from the Book of Acts that the Holy Spirit is *an abiding presence and not just an instantaneous quick fix.*

28

Since the Holy Spirit is a person His work is not mechanical but relational. He does not meet us at the altar with some kind of internal windup device like a spiritual clock that will be sufficient strength for all our problems for the rest of our lives by the sheer force of an internal mainspring. If we are going to use the analogy of the clock to help explain the sanctified life, let's use the electric clock, plugged into a source of power that is equal on a moment-by-moment basis for all the currents of concern and challenge in our lives. The sanctifying grace of God does not come from a celestial storage battery that is big enough to last all our lives. Our relationship to the Holy Spirit is more like a live connection with a generating source that continually creates power as needed.

John Wesley believed the work of the Holy Spirit was lifelong and divided into five different levels. (1) First, there is *prevenient grace,* which gives us the capacity to respond to the voice of God. (2) As prevenient grace is cultivated, it leads us into a *keen awareness of sin,* which is sometimes referred to as Holy Ghost conviction. (3) Then comes the *new birth,* which is wrought by the Spirit and is dependent on the Spirit. "If any man have not the Spirit of Christ, he is none of his" (Rom. 8:9). (4) After conversion comes, in due time, the hunger for a *deeper spiritual work.* This natural spiritual hunger is not confined within certain denominational lines. In the heart of every born-again believer there develops this hunger for a deeper work. You may call it full consecration, perfect love, baptism with the Holy Spirit, or whatever. Many theologians think this experience with the Holy Spirit following regeneration is most accurately called entire sanctification. (5) There is the ongoing *sanctifying grace of God that keeps on working in our lives* as we continue our pilgrimage with Him. It was 10 years after Pentecost when the Holy Spirit helped Peter get rid of his prejudice against Gentiles so he could preach to Cornelius and be God's agent when the Holy Spirit was poured out on the Gentile family of a Roman soldier in the army of occupation.

When Jesus taught His disciples about the Holy Spirit He told them, "If ye love me, keep my commandments. And I will pray the Father, and he shall give you another Comforter that he may *abide with you for ever*" (John 14:15-16). The Holy Spirit is God's Agent in the instantaneous experience of entire sanctification, but He is more than that. He is the abiding presence of God in our lives, our inner gyroscope for direction, and the generator of strength and the source of wisdom we need for staying on top of life.

Victor and Not a Victim

Finally, the Book of Acts teaches us that the Holy Spirit is the Victor and not the victim of our cultural conditioning. There are two great factors that dominate our behavior and create our personality. One is the physical self, and the other is the environment in which the person lives. Our physical characteristics come from the genes, while the conditioning that makes us think and act the way we do comes mostly from our interaction with our environment. Each of these personality factors is so great that many debates have been waged on whether the biological factor or the factor of cultural conditioning we get from our environment is the most powerful in shaping our lives and our behavior.

The genes determine the color of our eyes, the way our hair grows, our intelligence, physical stamina, and all the other biological factors that make you, you and me, me.

30

But that's not all. You are whatever you are today because of all that has happened to you from the day you were born until this moment, and maybe even more importantly, the way you have learned to respond or react to everything that has ever happened to you.

When do you start to train a child? The answer is, "Fifty years before he is born." By the time you can speak the language of the culture into which you were born, you're the victim of it.

For a moment I want you to imagine a church board in a congregation of 200 members in a town of 40,000 where several manufacturing plants have expanded and brought in many new blue-collar and white-collar people from other areas of the country. All these people are represented in the church and on the board. And like any good board they operate by committees. The chairman of the finance committee grew up in a townhouse in New York City. He has been conditioned by plenty of money all his life. He has a master's degree in business administration from Harvard Business School and serves as comptroller of his company where he handles great sums of money. However, I forgot to tell you that the treasurer of his church is a retired farmer who has been a member of the local church since 1932. The chairperson of the social committee is a computer programmer who grew up in North Hollywood and is just turning 30. The evangelism committee is chaired by a good ol' boy who has more zeal than wisdom and sees the ideal church as a year-round camp meeting. The chairman of the music committee has a degree from the American Conservatory and is in charge of music in the local high school. But the pianist can only play by ear, and the people would rather sing a southern gospel song than a Charles Wesley hymn.

You can use your imagination to see what their board meetings are like. They may all be saved and sanctified, but it is going to take some very special work of the Holy Spirit for these people to work together.

And here is the real problem: *The values and priorities I have are obviously the ones God intended all of you to have.* So anyone to my left is a hopeless liberal, and anyone to my right is a reactionary conservative.·

Only with the outpoured presence of the Holy Spirit can we learn to be victors and not victims of our cultural conditioning. Perhaps this is why all of us should sing the prayer Mrs. Mildred Cope put to music in our hymnbook:

> *Holy Spirit, my heart yearns for Thee;*
> *Holy Spirit, abide in me.*
> *Make me clean; oh, make me pure!*
> *I must know the double cure!*
> *Holy Spirit, be my Guide.*
> *Holy Spirit, my door's open wide.*
> *Make me to know Thy will divine;*
> *Holy Spirit, be Thou mine!**
>
> —MILDRED COPE

The Holy Spirit wants to be the abiding Presence in our lives who teaches us how to understand and live with the cultural conditioning that often drives us apart.

Chapter 3

Human Nature and Carnal Nature

Scriptural Stepping-stones

Spiritually minded . . . the carnal mind

> *For they that are after the flesh do mind the things of the flesh; but they that are after the Spirit the things of the Spirit. For to be carnally minded is death; but to be spiritually minded is life and peace. Because the carnal mind is enmity against God: for it is not subject to the law of God, neither indeed can be. So then they that are in the flesh cannot please God. But ye are not in the flesh, but in the Spirit, if so be that the Spirit of God dwell in you. Now if any man have not the Spirit of Christ, he is none of his.*

Rom. 8:5-9

A lot of inner conflict within Christians would go up in thin air if we all understood the difference between carnal nature and human nature. I have heard preachers give scathing denunciations of Christian behavior whose dynamics were no more than natural human responses. And I have heard Christians excuse their carnal behavior by calling it human.

What is the difference, then, between human nature and carnal nature? Human nature is that part of man's personality

33

that is rooted in his biological structure. This structure includes such things as the glands, a basic sex drive, and the mental capacity to make judgments. These and other characteristics of the human organism are neither carnal nor spiritual; they are human.

The human system of biological glands was computerized by the Creator to respond automatically to the changing faces of the environment. A strong threat or an attack of fear will cause the heart to pump faster and redden the face, beginning with warmness under the collar and a flushing of the skin starting at the collar line and coming up behind the ears and across the forehead and down the face. I have heard people call this flushed face syndrome carnal. But it isn't. It is the capillaries near the skin filled with more blood than usual as the heart pumps at a faster rate. People with light skin show red more than people with a swarthy skin. And some people, for biological reasons, show no redness at all.

One of the positive factors in life would be greatly diminished and the human race would eventually die out if there were not a sexual attraction between men and women. But the sex drive is human and of itself is neither carnal nor spiritual.

The mind is every man's computer to be programmed for good or evil. And the mind's ability to spot weaknesses, identify strengths, and see long-range consequences is all God-given. Therefore the prudence of budgeting, planning, buying insurance protection for your family, or using the services of a doctor is not a carnal lack of faith, because God gave us the mental equipment for these judgments in the first place. These and all the other human qualities with which God endowed man are a part of every person's human nature.

Of themselves human characteristics are neither carnal nor spiritual; they are a part of being human. God built this equipment into the human psyche and equipped the body to respond to the signals of the mind. It all happened when God said, "Let us make man in our image" (Gen. 1:26).

I find it most interesting that all of the human emotions —hate, depression, anger, jealousy, wrath, peace, love, and joy —are also ascribed to God in the Bible. God is a Spirit with a mind, emotions, and a will. It was the mind of God who became a person in Christ Jesus. It is the emotions of God that put positive and negative feelings into His universe. And it is the will of God that acts in history from the deliverance of the children of Israel from Egypt up to and including the ways He impacts the little world you and I live in today. These three qualities—mind, emotions, and will—are the spirit of man as God made him.

What, then, is carnal nature? Our personality is the sum total of everything that makes us who we are. This includes our physical body, the environment in which we were raised, and most of all, our inner spirit. And to paraphrase Paul, "Now abideth these three—the physical body, the surrounding environment, and the inner self—but the greatest of these is man's inner spirit" (1 Cor. 13:13).

The spirit is made carnal by the nature of indwelling sin. This sin—which demonstrates itself most fully in acts of unmitigated selfishness—perverts the mind, distorts the emotions, and nullifies the will. When the mind is perverted, the sex drive loses all its beauty and joy and is turned against itself, jading the personality and creating a sense of emptiness. The result is a desire for more pervertedness with ultimate disregard for the laws of human nature, family sanctity, and civil codes.

When the mind is carnal, the emotions rage out of control and find their main force in negative reactions. The ability to say, "Thank you," or, "I am sorry," has long since died in a human spirit or in a church that has lost its capacity to love. Hurting other people becomes a matter of little or no concern as someone walks out, destroys a good person by character assassination, and spreads his negativism and cynicism everywhere he goes, like a car polluting the air with its exhaust.

But there is another option, the Spirit-filled personality. The flawed character of the human body cannot be improved much by trying health foods, exercise, or plastic surgery. But the way we think about ourselves can be radically altered from negative to positive by a sanctified personality. Each of us is the victim of all that has ever happened to us from 50 years before we were born. We can't change our childhood experiences by covering them up with bitter thoughts. But through the sanctified personality we can change the way we feel about them. We may feel victimized by the people and the circumstances that surround us this moment. But we do not need to facilitate their possible power to hurt us by allowing our will to be paralyzed. The sanctified personality is not dependent on a beautiful, strong body, a childhood full of happy memories, a support system around us consisting of people who come up to our high standards, or circumstances that alleviate the complications of our daily living. The sanctified personality is cleansed, transformed, and empowered for joyful living.

Why settle for fun when you can be happy, and why settle for happiness when you can be fulfilled? This concept of a sanctified personality is espoused with psychological jargon by professional students of human nature. But it is expressed better by Paul nearly two millennia before the study of human nature became a matter of scholarly concern. Paul wrote, "Those who let themselves be controlled by their lower natures live only to please themselves, but those who follow after the Holy Spirit find themselves doing those things that please God. . . . You are controlled by your new nature if you have the Spirit living in you" (Rom. 8:5, 9, TLB).

Chapter *4*

The Sanctified Personality

Scriptural Stepping-stones

No condemnation . . .

> *There is therefore now no condemnation to them which are in Christ Jesus, who walk not after the flesh, but after the Spirit. For the law of the Spirit of life in Christ Jesus hath made me free from the law of sin and death. . . . That the righteousness of the law might be fulfilled in us, who walk not after the flesh, but after the Spirit.*

Rom. 8:1-2, 4

* * *

Life and peace . . .

> *For to be carnally minded is death; but to be spiritually minded is life and peace. . . . But if the Spirit of him that raised up Jesus from the dead dwell in you, he that raised up Christ from the dead shall also quicken your mortal bodies by his Spirit that dwelleth in you. . . . The Spirit itself beareth witness with our spirit, that we are the children of God.*

Rom. 8:6, 11, 16

Flesh and *Spirit* are two words that flash on and off like signal lights on the front of a presidential limousine as we roll through the first 17 verses of the 8th chapter of Romans. *Flesh* is used 12 times in this paragraph and *Spirit* 15 times.

The Roman believers in the Christian ghetto of the world's greatest city understood these words, *flesh* and *Spirit,* fully. But before we can talk much about a sanctified personality, we need to know what they mean. In our informal conversation *flesh* either means the human point of view or, literally, the flesh on the bone. Paul uses *flesh* in both these common meanings. He speaks of circumcision "in the flesh" (Rom. 2:28), which is an obvious reference to cutting away the physical flesh. And he speaks of Jesus as the Son of David "according to the flesh" (1:3), which is the lineage of Jesus from the human point of view.

But Paul has a spiritual use for the word *flesh* that is all his own. The word *flesh* stands for the depraved side of man's personality. A man is carnal when he walks after the flesh (Rom. 3:5). Man is weak "through the flesh" (8:3*a*). God sent His Son "in the likeness of sinful flesh" (v. 3*b*). There is no way people who are "in the flesh" (v. 3*c*) can please God. All of these statements are true because the old sinful nature within us is "against God" (v. 7). The depraved personality is dominated by a mind that distorts reality for its own selfish purposes. The depraved personality is motivated by negative reactive emotions like malice, destructive jealousy, and cynicism. The carnal outlook assumes everybody has his price and every situation can be manipulated. The depraved personality is guided by a weak will that is subject to peer pressure and is always the victim of the times we're in.

Unfortunately, the carnal personality in our culture is accepted as normal. The carnal mind has an ample store of rationalizations for evil thoughts and deeds. We really do believe everybody is doing it, and it must be right or I wouldn't have these urges and desires. Our culture has even developed a whole system of ethics to accommodate the carnal mind. Something is only right or wrong according to the situation, and there are no moral absolutes. And we have a philosophy to go with our situation ethics called existentialism. I am for me, and whatever meets my needs and satisfies my feelings is right for me. If it feels good, do it. And with two consenting adults, anything goes. The results of the carnal mind are a moral breakdown in the culture, education without values, the home without sanctity, and life without meaning. The impact of the carnal mind in our culture is worse than the results of an atomic war on our planet. The flesh, as Paul uses the term, is not something to take lightly; it is the avenger of Satan.

The second great word in this paragraph is *Spirit.* In the Old Testament, the word *Spirit* was sometimes the powerful and mysterious Word of God. It was the Spirit who "moved upon the face of the waters" (Gen. 1:2) in creation. And it was this kind of powerful, life-giving word the Christians heard and felt at Pentecost.

For Paul, the Spirit is the divine power from God that comes to cleanse and liberate a man's personality from the domination of the carnal nature. Life in the Spirit frees a man from his depraved nature and gives him power to live by.

However, defining and contrasting flesh and Spirit are not the full answer to the meaning of the sanctified personality. There is one other element to face in human personality besides the option between freedom from sin and the fullness of the Spirit. Even after the mind has been liberated from sin, each of us is still human. No one resigns the human race when he is sanctified. Since carnality abides in the will, the will of man can be cleansed of inbred sin and made pure in love.

41

Even then, our appetites, our needs for recognition, the urge for survival, and all the other needs in human nature are still very much alive. But our responses to these needs are sanctified responses.

However, it is important to understand that these sanctified responses are not automatic. Entire sanctification is an event, consummated in an instant. But sanctification is also a process. The sanctified life is not a 100-yard dash. It is more like a cross-country run. It is not like an alarm clock set in irreversible motion by a winding device in the back that must be attended only when it runs down. If sanctification is going to be compared to a clock, it must be an electric clock plugged into a source that supplies the amount of power needed for the day. Because we are human the sanctified personality is both a moment of beginning and a lifelong process. Because we are human and because we are filled with the Spirit we are ready for our personality to develop along the lines of the seven blessings in the first 17 verses of Romans 8.

Free from Condemnation

First, the sanctified personality is free from condemnation. "There is therefore now *no condemnation* to them which are in Christ Jesus, who walk not after the flesh, but after the Spirit" (v. 1).

Guilt and condemnation are as devastating to the human personality as bankruptcy is to an American businessman. Feelings of guilt change a personality because guilt changes the way we think about ourselves. And anything that changes the way we think about ourselves changes our personality.

Through the years I have watched students who have been caught breaking the college code. Some try to deny it. And if lying doesn't work because of irrefutable evidence, they will almost always attack the process by which they were caught and condemned. They have their version of the old-fashioned cartoon that showed the motorcycle policeman hiding behind the billboard waiting to catch the speeder. And the message is clear that the policeman's method is more reprehensible than the excess speed of the motorist. The condemned motorist would like to transfer guilt from himself to the policeman who caught him. Only once in a while is there a student who admits, "I did it. I don't know why. It was not like me. What do you want me to do?" Sanctified honesty about ourselves and our predicament does something positive in the personality.

The sanctified Christian is still human and subject to mistakes. But there is no need to feel guilty and condemned by my inept emotions or the limitations in my judgments, which are always more obvious to others than to me. The complicating factor in our failures is the judgmental attitude of our detractors. But even here, the fulfilled person can be free from condemnation. No one can make you feel inadequate unless you allow him to.

The sanctified Christian does not further complicate his existence by projecting the cause of his problems on others, by lashing out in unchristian terms and tones, or by making public or private promises to strike back at the person who is the agent of distress. The sanctified personality glows in the heat of discord by affirming the grace of God in forgiveness and by practicing the presence of Jesus in attitudes that heal instead of hurt.

Free from the Vicious Cycle

Second, the sanctified personality is free from "the vicious circle [cycle] of sin and death" (Rom. 8:2, TLB). "For what *the law was powerless* to do in ... the sinful nature, *God did by sending his own Son* ... in order that the righteous requirements of the law might be fully met in us, who *do not live according to the sinful nature but according to the Spirit"* (vv. 3-4, NIV).

For many people, the cycle of sin and death applies to the grave and what happens thereafter. But there are other ways the law of sin and death applies here on earth during the process of living. For instance, there can be death to what we might have been. I saw a teenager destroy himself in only a few years by the sin in his rebellion against his parents and all other symbols of authority. A loving, happy boy became a hard, harsh young adult with lines on his face to prove it. The sorrow that came to many of us who watched the process was his death to what might have been a useful life.

There is also death to a good marriage and a happy family. The carnal nature, which distorts the human personality, will bring havoc into a home. Living death is often worse than physical death. But freedom from the destructive forces in personality comes when the Christian is made free by the indwelling presence of the Spirit.

Fulfilled

Third, the sanctified personality is the key to the fulfilled life: "That ... righteousness might be fulfilled in us" (Rom. 8:4).

The righteousness that fulfills our lives is *not self-righteousness.* Feeling high and mighty about ourselves is the devil's way of getting us ready for a hard fall. Furthermore, self-righteousness is a negative witness for Christ because it turns people away from the faith that brings true righteousness. The righteousness that fulfills our lives is *not ethical righteousness.* You may keep all of the written and unwritten law in your church to the satisfaction of everyone and still fail to enjoy the fulfilled life. The righteousness that fulfills our lives is *not legal perfection* in personal righteousness.

God's righteousness *is the loving relationship* God has toward us who are undeserving. And our righteousness comes by faith in Christ, who teaches us and *empowers us to a loving relationship with God and with each other.* Love is the substance that fulfills life and makes a personality attractive.

Life and Peace

Fourth, the sanctified personality lives at peace: "For to be carnally minded is death; but *to be spiritually minded is life and peace"* (Rom. 8:6). Or, as a paraphrase puts it, "Following after the Holy Spirit leads to life and peace, but following after the old nature leads to death, because the old sinful nature within us is against God" (vv. 6-7, TLB).

Nothing drains the strength out of a personality faster than turmoil. Many people are exhausted from fighting themselves. Jealousy, maliciousness, strife, and dissension are projected into life's situations by people who are torn inside by their own jealousy, malice, strife, and dissension. For instance, people who criticize you are not trying to make you a

45

better person; they are projecting their own unhappiness on you. They are not trying to meet your needs but theirs. There is beauty in the Christian personality, which demonstrates the vitality of patience, gentleness, and self-control. These characteristics of a loving personality only surface in the person who is at peace with himself and with God.

Vitality

Fifth, the sanctified personality is possessed by mental and emotional vitality: "And if the Spirit . . . is living in you, he . . . *will also give life to your mortal bodies* through his Spirit" (Rom. 8:11, NIV).

There are two reasons why I believe God gives us physical energies beyond ourselves at times when we need it. Nothing drains off our energy and saps our strength faster than being torn on the inside. The double-minded man is not only unstable but worn out as well. If you don't believe it, just look around at all the people who are burning up all their strength fighting themselves. Since the sanctified Christian has his life put together he has an energy advantage over the carnal personality. And second, the sanctified Christian will generate more energy just because he is free from the negative drag of hostility, self-centeredness, and self-pity. The more carnal baggage you insist on carrying, the faster you wear out. A clean mind and a pure heart are God's channels for continuing strength. Energy begets energy in the life that is free from carnal attitudes.

Sixth, the sanctified personality has the strength to control itself: "If ye live after the flesh, ye shall die: but if ye through the Spirit do *mortify the deeds of the body, ye shall live"* (Rom. 8:13).

God does not do for us what we can do for ourselves. He will cleanse our will, but we still make our own decisions. He will cleanse the fountainhead of our emotions, but we still are left the responsibility of controlling our emotions. The body may call for food and drink, but through our will we control how much we eat and what we drink. The body may call for sexual gratification, but each person has the responsibility to meet these needs within the limits of God's directives, which have been spelled out in many places in the Bible. The sanctified Christian does not have a passive personality, but in Christ he does have the strength and the will to do what is right.

Bondage and Fear

And finally, the sanctified personality is free from the spirit of bondage and fear: "For *ye have not received the spirit of bondage* again *to fear; but ye have received the Spirit of adoption,* whereby we cry, Abba, Father. The Spirit itself beareth witness with our spirit, that we are the children of God" (Rom. 8:15-16).

Adoption was serious business in the Roman world and was often used as a means for keeping the family name alive when there was no natural-born son. The adopted child became a son in every sense of the legal relationship including his name and his inheritance. But he also became a son emotionally. "Abba" actually means "Daddy." The adopted father of the son was not an austere head of the family but a person

47

whom the boy felt comfortable calling "Daddy." The loving father had a loving son, and between them they had a loving relationship. That is the picture of the Spirit-filled Christian and the Heavenly Father.

People who are alienated, lonely, and lacking a feeling of self-worth almost always show it in their personality. They are fearful and under bondage because they feel unloved. This is opposite the picture of the Christian who loves and is loved, comfortable in the presence of God and in the presence of God's people. This is the sanctified personality—the only way to live.

Chapter 5

The Illusion of Perfection

Many people who glibly say they believe in the Sermon on the Mount have never stopped to consider the meaning of Christ's call for perfection. Jesus commanded, "Be ye therefore perfect, even as your Father which is in heaven is perfect" (Matt. 5:48). That is the most startling and, as E. Stanley Jones put it, the most difficult saying Jesus ever made. It would have been enough if Jesus had ended His statement after His call for perfection. But He added a phrase that seems to make it all the more impossible. How can anyone in the world be perfect like God is perfect?

The context in which something was said is important for understanding the meaning of any quote. People have often been hurt by someone who lifted their words out of context and used them for different purposes than the spokesman intended. Some time ago I received a letter of criticism about one of the major administrators of our college. The person writing me was quoting something this man was supposed to have said. I read the letter and answered it before I ever put it down. I said, "I've never heard this man say what you think he said. I have never heard him say anything that sounded remotely like what you have quoted. And what you say that he has said doesn't sound like anything I would expect him to say. I have a feeling that somebody has taken what he said and lifted it out of context and distorted it just enough to serve his own purposes." I signed my name and sent the letter off. In less than a week I had back a cordial letter of apology telling me the quote was indeed lifted out of context and distorted enough to change its meaning.

Therefore, when Jesus said, "Be ye therefore perfect, even as your Father which is in heaven is perfect," we need to know the setting in which He said it. Jesus was teaching His disciples on a grassy knoll not far from the north shore of the Sea of Galilee, close to the ancient city of Capernaum. He was having what might be called discipling classes. Jesus was discipling the disciples. In modern language, Jesus was having a seminar to teach His disciples how to be better disciples. And in this series of sessions He expounded the hands-on issues of daily living. What we have in the Sermon on the Mount is probably an annotated outline of a much larger body of material that Jesus discussed with His inside people.

The themes and issues Jesus covered in these teachings can be divided into easily identified sections. (1) He began with the eight great principles for happiness known as the Beatitudes. It must have taken a long morning for Jesus to explain those revolutionary, mind-stretching ideas. (2) Jesus identified the qualities of a Kingdom man. He is like salt, like a city set on a hill, and like a lamp on a lampstand giving a warm glow to an otherwise dreary setting. (3) Then Jesus turned to the subject of the law and how it could be fulfilled. Jesus had no thought of doing away with the law: "I am not come to destroy, but to fulfill [the law]" (Matt. 5:17). Then He nailed down His own commitment to the law when He said, "Till heaven and earth pass, one jot or one tittle shall in no wise pass from the law" (v. 18). But He also made very clear that the law of itself was not sufficient: "Except your righteousness shall exceed the righteousness of the scribes and

Pharisees, ye shall in no case enter into the kingdom of heaven" (v. 20).

The significance and scope of this teaching must surely have spilled over into a second day or at least an afternoon session. Talking about murder, adultery, honesty, and revenge is heavy stuff, with many ramifications and implications. It was at the end of this discussion on the law that Jesus came to the royal law of love as a fulfilling principle and to His call for Christian perfection: "Be ye therefore *perfect,* even *as your Father which is in heaven* is perfect" (Matt. 5:48).

Absolute Perfection

However, getting the context in which Jesus called for perfection is only a beginning. There is still a lot of underbrush that gets in our way of accepting Christian perfection as the norm for our lives. *First is the hang-up we have over technical, or absolute, perfection.* We read about interplanetary explorations in equipment built by scientists who talk about tolerances in millionths of an inch. The degrees of technical perfection stagger our minds.

On Sunday afternoon, July 25, 1969, two men set down their spaceship in a valley of the moon and stepped out to say something about one small step for man and one giant step for mankind. To break the tension of that historic moment, I made a little joke with my wife about what Neil Armstrong would do if he got back into his landing vehicle to leave the moon and the battery was down. You know the answer. The men at NASA near Houston did not believe in the technical perfection of any machine. So they built multiple backup sys-

51

tems to cover their inevitable failures at striving for absolute perfection.

I rode from Lansing to the metropolitan airport in Detroit some time ago with the governor's chauffeur and bodyguard. En route, he told me about the new car that had been delivered to the governor of Michigan. Because he was governor of the state that specializes in the manufacture of automobiles, the Chrysler Corporation wanted him to have the ultimate, the *perfect* automobile. Everything in this automobile was operated by push buttons, electrically controlled and computerized. Everything but the steering worked automatically. Even the hood was raised and lowered by an electronic motor guaranteed to keep the driver from getting his hands dirty.

The perfect automobile ran without flaw except for one problem. On the second morning after the car was delivered, the battery was down. The button that was designed to activate the motor to raise the hood would not work because it was also battery powered. And unlike NASA's engineers, no one had thought of providing a backup system. The driver told me he tinkered with the hood, kicked the tires, and crawled underneath the car as his frustrations mounted; and the governor waited inside, looking at his watch and tapping the sill of the window with his fingers. A call to the engineers of Chrysler resulted in the suggestion that they take off the bumper. Finally, the engineers themselves came from Detroit to Lansing to see what could be done. And the driver told me that the last time he saw the perfect automobile, it was going down the road, pulled by a wrecker on its way back to the factory.

Now you and I identify with that story because we all know nothing is perfect. There is no such thing as absolute, technical perfection. Therefore, when Jesus said, "Be ye therefore perfect," He was not talking about absolute or technical perfection. They made wheels by hand and rode in ox carts and on the backs of burros when Jesus was telling His disciples to be perfect.

Human Perfection

Some more underbrush that needs to be cleared out of the way is the idea of *human perfection*. A perfectionist is difficult to live with. If you are married to a perfectionist who must keep a perfect house, who has an unreasonable standard for everyone's behavior, who has a place and a time and a system for everything, your work is cut out for you. And if you work with somebody who is a perfectionist, you know already that they never let you forget it when your humanity shows. That's just the way perfectionists are. But for most of us, we not only fail to be humanly perfect, we aren't even trying.

Distorted Perfection

The third kind of underbrush that needs to be swept out of the way is the idea of *distorted perfection*. There is a widely practiced distortion of Christian perfection that has turned off a lot of people from the way of holiness. I'm thinking now of a church I know very well. They are loud in their proclamations of holiness. They pride themselves in standards that are not even in the official discipline of the church. They call for emotional responses that are not scriptural and tend to stand in judgment on people who do not see things their way. Many have lost their own children to the church. They have developed a turned-off generation who have drifted away and have not come back.

This kind of spiritual distortion has some clear-cut characteristics. (1) The people are negative. (2) The people are legalistic. They believe in salvation by grace but just barely. (3) And invariably that church is dominated by one strong family, and that family is both negative and legalistic.

What, then, did Jesus mean by perfection? And why did He call His disciples to a life of Christian perfection? If we follow the principle Jesus used when He talked about the fulfillment of Old Testament law, we can know fully what Jesus meant when He called His people to perfection.

Chapter 6

The Meaning of Perfection

Scriptural Stepping-stones

Ye have heard . . . but I say . . .

> *Ye have heard . . . Thou shalt not commit adultery: But I say . . . whosoever looketh on a woman to lust after her hath committed adultery . . . already in his heart.*
>
> Matt. 5:27-28

> *Thou shalt not forswear [perjure] thyself . . . But I say . . . Swear not at all . . .*
>
> Matt. 5:33-34

> *. . . An eye for an eye, and a tooth for a tooth: But I say . . . That ye resist not evil . . .*
>
> Matt. 5:38-39

> *. . . Thou shalt love thy neighbour . . . But I say . . . love your enemies . . .*
>
> Matt. 5:43-44

*   *   *

Therefore perfect . . .

> *Be ye therefore perfect, even as your Father which is in heaven is perfect.*
>
> Matt. 5:48

*   *   *

Perfect purity

> *And if thy right eye offend thee, pluck it out, and cast it from thee: for it is profitable for thee that one of thy members should perish, and not that thy whole body should be cast into hell.*

Matt. 5:29

*   *   *

Perfect honesty

> *But let your communication be, Yea, yea; Nay, nay: for whatsoever is more than these cometh of evil.*

Matt. 5:37

*   *   *

Perfect forgiveness

> *Ye have heard that it hath been said, An eye for an eye, and a tooth for a tooth: but I say unto you, That ye resist not evil: but whosoever shall smite thee on thy right cheek, turn to him the other also.*

Matt. 5:38-39

*   *   *

Perfect love

> *For if ye love them which love you, what reward have ye? do not even the publicans the same? And if ye salute your brethren only, what do ye more than others? do not even the publicans so? Be ye therefore perfect, even as your Father which is in heaven is perfect.*

Matt. 5:46-48

What did Jesus mean when He called His disciples to be perfect? There are some things He surely did not mean. (1) Jesus was not calling for absolute perfection, because there is no such thing. (2) He was not asking for human perfection, for it does not exist. (3) He was certainly not calling for the distorted kind of holiness perfection that demonstrates self-righteousness, legalism, and emotionalism. What then did Jesus mean when He said to His disciples, "Be ye therefore perfect, even as your Father which is in heaven is perfect" (Matt. 5:48)?

There is a concept of perfection that explains what Jesus had in mind. It comes right out of the common sense of everyday living. It makes sense without the help of theologians or philosophers to explain it: That *person,* or that *situation,* or that *thing* is perfect *that fulfills the purpose for which it was created.*

Let me illustrate. I have a pen in my pocket that I just love. In fact, it's a perfect pen. It is a Cross felt-tipped pen made from sterling silver. On the clip it has the logo of the college I serve, beautifully crafted in the college colors. It always writes smoothly, never skipping or balking. And I love to use it. It was a gift presented to me on a ceremonial occasion, which makes it all the more cherished. It really is a perfect pen. It does for me everything a pen is supposed to do. However, it is the nature of sterling to dent easily, because it is a soft metal. And if you examine it closely, you can see a dent on the back side where I dropped it once on the edge of my desk. But that doesn't mean my pen is not still perfect, for it continues to fulfill beautifully the purpose for which it was created.

Look at it another way: On Thursday of this week, after all the trustees are safely on their way home from their May meeting here on campus, and I have finished the work that needs to be done to wrap up the school year, I am meeting my teenage son in Kansas City; and we are leaving on a journey in a four-wheel-drive Golden Eagle Jeep Cherokee from The Landing in Kansas City to follow the Old Oregon Trail all the way to the Falls in the Willamette River in Oregon. We are going to have an unforgettable time together. Les III keeps on saying to me, over and over, "Dad, I can hardly study. . . . I think about our trip all day, and I dream about it at night."

And I respond to him in all honesty, "Les, I am the same way. I find it a little harder to give myself to all that I am supposed to be doing this commencement season, for I am looking forward to that trip that we are going to have together in the Jeep."

I am not exaggerating when I say at least six persons have come to me at separate times in the last few days and said, "Dr. Parrott, that is absolutely the perfect father-and-son trip."

Or is it? My secretary gave me a tackle box for Christmas four years ago. I still have the red ribbon on it. But I am going to take off the ribbon and fill it with fishing gear. I have the promise of an experienced fisherman to take me to buy a rod and reel. My son already has his. We're going to enjoy fishing along the way.

But I have already conceded there will be flaws in the perfect father-and-son trip. We'll have mosquitoes, maybe a flat tire. We're going to fix some of our own meals even though I am well aware of my ineptness. But none of these potential problems will matter. They are only passing clouds in a perfect sky. That trip to Oregon will be the perfect father-and-son trip because it will fulfill all the things that he and I had in mind when we came up with the idea.

Let me open one more window to let in light on this concept of perfection in fulfillment of purpose. There is a faculty member in our college whom I consider to be the perfect ideal of a professor on a Christian campus. I can't help it; I just automatically judge prospective faculty by the sterling standards he has set in academic credentials, quality teaching, and Christian life-style. He fulfills all I believe it takes to be the perfect professor for our college.

But that doesn't mean that he is without flaw. I was in a meeting not long ago where he disagreed with me. That is not a fatal error, but it did give me pause for thought. I watched him make an administrative decision last year I felt was wrong, but I did not intervene. And we've been coping with the negative consequences of it ever since. But that does not change the fact. To me he's the perfect professor for our institution because he fulfills all that a professor is supposed to be in this kind of college.

Now let's face the hard part of this concept of Christian perfection. What about God? God is perfect because God is absolutely without any flaw. He makes no mistakes. But God is perfect for another reason. God is perfect because God fulfills all that God is supposed to be. That means that He is all-powerful. He is everywhere at the same time. He is holy. He is without sin. He is loving, just, compassionate, and sensitive. He has every characteristic that belongs to himself. God has these characteristics because God is God, and in Him is the fulfillment of all that God is ever supposed to be.

Edgar Sheffield Brightman, in his book on the philosophy of religion, calls these characteristics "the given in God." These are those qualities in God that cannot be taken from Him. Without them He is not God. Therefore, you and I can be perfect in Christ as we fulfill God's purpose in our lives.

You and I can only fulfill the law in our hearts when our hearts have been filled with the love of Jesus Christ. He said, "Ye have heard that it hath been said, Thou shalt love thy neighbour, and hate thine enemy. But I say unto you, Love your enemies, bless them that curse you. . . . your Father . . . sendeth rain on the just and on the unjust" (Matt. 5:43-45). He loves everybody.

You and I can never fulfill the purpose for which we were created until we have come to the point of unconditional love. And unconditional love comes from God through His Son Jesus Christ and is effected within us by the dominating power of the Holy Spirit. This is impossible in both experience and theology except for the cleansing work of the Holy Spirit.

In the beginning God made man and gave him a home in the Garden of Eden. God's purpose was for man to live in perfect fellowship with Him. God came down in the cool of the day and walked and talked with Adam and Eve as they lived in fellowship together. But for love to be genuine and not self-serving, there had to be the option not to love. God gave man the option of demonstrating love to Him by refraining from the fruit of the tree of good and evil. Adam and Eve, as it were, shook their fists in the face of God and declared, "We'll have our own will rather than Yours." And they were alienated from God.

This disobedience made man self-conscious over his relationship with God, and as a defensive measure, Adam and Eve tried to hide. That's when they became self-conscious over their nakedness and wove aprons of leaves to cover themselves. Man was cast out of the Garden of Eden, alienated from God, alienated from himself, and alienated from his brothers and sisters by his own mind of self-centeredness. It wasn't long until the first family was devastated by the terrible murder within their own household, one brother killing another.

God's purpose as revealed in the Bible was to bring back man into that fellowship he lost by disobedience. And in a mysterious way none of us can fully explain, "God was in Christ, reconciling the world unto himself" (2 Cor. 5:19). It is possible for us to live in a deep, abiding fellowship of love with God in Christ. The fulfillment of this love relationship is Christian perfection, for this is the purpose for which God made us. And this is why Jesus said, "Be ye therefore perfect, even as your Father which is in heaven is perfect" (Matt. 5:48).

You can be perfect and still be human. About a generation ago, or a little more, the eloquent, silver-tongued camp meeting preacher Raymond Browning was preaching at a huge camp meeting site near Columbus, Ohio. Following a service of unusual blessing in which one of his colleagues had preached, Raymond Browning sat down under one of those venerable shade trees and sketched the words in his mind into a marvelous song. It has been lost to most gospel singers for a long time. But the other day, I heard it for the first time in many years to the blessing of all.

Dark the sin that soiled man's nature;
Long the distance that he fell,
Far removed from hope and heaven,
Near to deep despair and hell.
But there was a fountain opened,
And the blood of God's own Son
Purifies the soul, and reaches
*Deeper than the stain has gone.** *

Don't be destroyed by the scoffers who distort the meaning of Christian holiness by confusing it with absolute perfection or human perfection. Let God's Holy Spirit cleanse your mind and activate your will for the living Presence that helps us fulfill the royal law of love in our relationships with Him and with each other.

Chapter 7

The Fullness of Life

Somewhere in the files of the Alumni Office in Oxford University is the name of John Wesley. Wesley attended Oxford from 1720 to 1724 for an undergraduate degree, and again in 1726 and 1727 for graduate study. He had a lifelong love affair with his alma mater, for he wrote when he was 78 years old, "I love the very sight of Oxford."

Visitors to Oxford today may be shown an upstairs room on the south side of the quadrangle where John Wesley lived and studied. Although the room today is occupied by a student, it contains Wesley's bust. And it doesn't take much imagination to feel his ghost about the place.

Only a short distance from Wesley's room is the college church of Oxford, called the Church of St. Mary. Many historic persons and events have come together in this church with its great spire, which dominates the skyline of Oxford. It was here that John Wycliffe denounced the clerical abuses of the 14th century. From its pulpit, Pusey gave his scholarly sermons and Newman cast the spell of his irresistible personality over the listening throngs who came to hear him preach.

It was also here in the sanctuary of this university church that alumnus John Wesley of the class of 1724, and now a tutor, was asked to preach. The time was August 24, 1744. Wesley was 41 years of age.

For Wesley, this occasion was an epoch-making event. The colorful academic march moved to the sound of a great organ. When the procession came to the front of the church, the vice-chancellor nodded for Mr. Wesley to ascend the pulpit stairs while the others took their appointed places in the reserved pews. The order of worship was simple. There was an opening hymn, followed by the morning prayer; then without introduction, Wesley stood to speak.

John Wesley would have looked strange by today's standards. Only 5 feet 6 inches tall, he must have looked diminutive in that exalted pulpit. His outer garment was an Oxford robe, and after the fashion of his day, he wore a flowing wig with the hair rolled about his shouders. He wore knee britches (breeches) and had buckles on his shoes. If his appearance might have seemed strange to us, however, his message would not. With a strong, self-amplified voice, John Wesley announced his text and preached from Acts 4:31, "And they were all filled with the Holy Ghost."

John Wesley began his sermon by describing the power of the Holy Spirit in the lives of those in Jerusalem who received the first outpourings of the Spirit. Then he told how the Holy Spirit was received by others as Christianity moved across the world, making his point that the Spirit was not limited to those original disciples but was available to Christians of every generation in every land. Then in the final portion of his sermon, Wesley applied his message by making an impassioned plea for the presence of scriptural Christianity on the campus of Oxford.

The sermon got an immediate reaction. The vice-chancellor sent for a copy of the manuscript. The sermon offended many and caused no small stir in the campus community. But Mr. Wesley left the commotion behind as he rode off on horseback 25 miles that afternoon to keep his evening preaching appointment. Wesley continued to love his alma mater, but after his message on scriptural Christianity, John Wesley was never again invited to preach in the university church.

The sermon that the religious humanists found revolting was not given to Wesley in one flashing moment of spiritual insight. Nor was it ground out in a quiet cloister of Lincoln College. John Wesley was a practical man, not a theorist. Wesley was an Anglican churchman who never planned to leave the fold. He was an evangelist who preached on hillsides and in open fields to the common people who felt uncomfortable in the churches. He was a scholar who taught at Oxford and wrote scores of books and hundreds of pamphlets. He even made his own translation of the New Testament. He was a group therapist who used shock treatments 200 years ahead of his time.

This many-faceted Christian genius hammered out his theology on three anvils over a period of years. His first anvil was Scripture. He always asked, "What does the Bible say?" At one point he described himself as a man of one book, the Bible. His second anvil was intellectual understanding. Doctrine for Wesley had to pass the test of logic and common sense. His third anvil was human experience. "Does this doctrine fit the facts of life?" Someone asked Wesley what he would do if he found a truth in the Bible that did not work in human experience. His answer was that he would go back to the Bible and start reading again.

Wesley found in Scripture and in life the central reality of the New Testament Church, that the Comforter who is the

Holy Spirit had come and abides in the minds and hearts of believers who are open to Him. Wesley's message to the students and faculty of Oxford was plain and understandable: (1) All those believers in Jerusalem were filled with the Holy Spirit. (2) Millions of believers beyond and since Jerusalem have been filled with the Holy Spirit. (3) And all of you on Oxford's faculty and in the student body may be filled with the Holy Spirit. Wesley wished he could say of his alma mater, "And they were all filled with the Holy Ghost" (Acts 4:31).

There is no doubt the Holy Spirit was a central reality in the narrative of the first-generation Christians in Acts. The references to the Holy Spirit coming as a special event are too many to ignore: (1) On the Day of Pentecost, *"They were all filled with the Holy Ghost"* (Acts 2:4). (2) When Peter and John returned from jail, forbidden by the Sanhedrin to speak or heal in the name of Jesus, they had a very earnest prayer with all the Christians of Jerusalem, *"And they were all filled with the Holy Ghost"* (4:31). (3) When the Christians were looking for lay leadership on the first church board, *"they chose Stephen, a man full of faith and of the Holy Ghost"* (6:5). (4) When Peter and John ministered to the new converts in the Samaritan revival, they *"laid their hands on them, and they received the Holy Ghost"* (8:17). (5) The message of Ananias to Saul following his Damascus Road experience was, "Brother Saul, the Lord, even Jesus, that appeared unto thee in the way as thou camest, hath sent me, that thou mightest receive thy sight, and *be filled with the Holy Ghost"* (9:17). (6) Even the Jews who traveled with Peter when he preached to the family of Cornelius "were astonished" (10:45) at the results of his ministry. "While Peter yet spake these words, *the Holy Ghost fell on them which heard the word"* (10:44). (7)

Peter later reported the event to the council in Jerusalem. "And God, which knoweth the hearts, bare them witness, *giving them the Holy Ghost, even as he did unto us;* and put no difference between us and them, purifying their hearts by faith" (15:8-9). (8) When Paul visited the church in Ephesus, he asked them, "Have ye received the Holy Ghost since ye believed?" They responded by saying, "We have not so much as heard whether there be any Holy Ghost. . . . And when Paul had laid his hands on them, *the Holy Ghost came on them"* (19:2, 6).

Through 1,900 years the focus of the church has shifted from the Holy Spirit to such concerns as orthodoxy, liturgy, expansionism, churchmanship, and political power. But in every era there have always been those sincere followers of the Lord who have been filled with the vital presence of the Holy Spirit. To deny the work of the Holy Spirit is to deny the Trinity and the authority of the Bible, and to ignore the witness of millions. "For the promise is unto you, and to your children, and to all that are afar off" (Acts 2:39).

The Big Difference

The question that plagues the minds of practical Christians in a high tech society is, "What difference does the Holy Spirit make in men's lives today?" And the answer is, "He makes the same difference in lives now as He did among the first-generation Christians."

My method of study in this regard is simplistic. I read through Acts with a yellow pad of paper by my side and lift out the obvious things that happened when people were filled with the Holy Spirit.

1. They became *powerful witnesses:* "But ye shall receive power, after that the Holy Ghost is come upon you: and ye shall be witnesses unto me both in Jerusalem, and in all Judaea, and in Samaria, and unto the uttermost part of the earth" (1:8).

2. They experienced a *miracle in communications:* "And they were all filled with the Holy Ghost, and began to speak with other tongues, as the Spirit gave them utterance. And there were dwelling at Jerusalem Jews, devout men, out of every nation under heaven. . . . and were confounded, because that every man heard them speak in his own language" (2:4-6).

3. They demonstrated an *enduring commitment:* "And they continued stedfastly in the apostles' doctrine and fellowship, and in breaking of bread, and in prayers" (2:42).

4. They enjoyed a *reverential trust* and a *hatred of evil:* "And fear came upon every soul" (2:43*a*).

5. *Miracles became real:* "And many wonders and signs were done by the apostles" (2:43*b*).

6. They had strong *concern for each other:* "And all that believed were together, and had all things common; and sold their possessions and goods, and parted them to all men, as every man had need" (2:44-45).

7. They *lived in a happy accord* with God and with each other: "And they, continuing daily with one accord in the temple, and breaking bread from house to house, did eat their meat with gladness and singleness of heart, praising God, and having favour with all the people. And the Lord added to the church daily such as should be saved" (2:46-47).

8. They learned how to depend on the Holy Spirit in *coping with stress:* "And now, Lord, behold their threatenings: and grant unto thy servants, that with all boldness they may speak thy word, . . . and they were all filled with the Holy Ghost, and they spake the word of God with boldness" (4:29, 31).

9. They experienced a *spirit of unity* that was more powerful than their differences: "And the multitude of them that believed were of one heart and of one soul: neither said any of them that aught of the things which he possessed was his own; but they had all things common" (4:32).

10. They experienced a *gracious power to witness:* "And with great power gave the apostles witness of the resurrection of the Lord Jesus: and great grace was upon them all" (4:33).

11. They experienced the *power to forgive* under the worst circumstances: "And they stoned Stephen, calling upon God, and saying, Lord Jesus, receive my spirit. And he kneeled down, and cried with a loud voice, Lord, lay not this sin to their charge. And when he had said this, he fell asleep" (7:59-60).

12. They developed quiet *patience in the face of conflict* and confusion: "And when Saul was come to Jerusalem, he assayed to join himself to the disciples: but they were all afraid of him, and believed not that he was a disciple" (9:26).

13. The fountainhead of their *inner life was purified:* "And God, which knoweth the hearts, bare them witness, giving them the Holy Ghost, even as he did unto us; and put no difference between us and them, purifying their hearts by faith" (15:8-9).

14. They learned to count on the Holy Spirit for *daily guidance:* "Now when they had gone throughout Phrygia and the region of Galatia, and were forbidden of the Holy Ghost to preach the word in Asia, after they were come to Mysia, they assayed to go into Bithynia: but the Spirit suffered them not. And they passing by Mysia came down to Troas. And a vision appeared to Paul in the night; There stood a man of Macedonia, and prayed him, saying, Come over into Macedonia, and help us. And after he had seen the vision, immediately we endeavoured to go into Macedonia, assuredly gathering that the Lord had called us for to preach the gospel unto them" (16:6-10).

15. They learned how to *sing during the midnights of life:* "And at midnight Paul and Silas prayed, and sang praises unto God: and the prisoners heard them. And suddenly there was a great earthquake, so that the foundations of the prison were shaken: and immediately all the doors were opened, and every one's bands were loosed" (16:25-26).

16. They became *instruments of healing:* "And God wrought special miracles by the hands of Paul: so that from his body were brought unto the sick handkerchiefs or aprons, and the diseases departed from them, and the evil spirits went out of them" (19:11-12).

17. They *lost their need for trashy literature:* "Many of them also which used curious arts brought their books together, and burned them before all men: and they counted the price of them, and found it fifty thousand pieces of silver. So mightily grew the word of God and prevailed" (19:19-20).

18. They *discarded all the gods made with hands:* "For a certain man named Demetrius, a silversmith, which made

silver shrines for Diana, brought no small gain unto the craftsmen; whom he called together with the workmen of like occupation, and said, Sirs, ye know that by this craft we have our wealth. Moreover ye see and hear, that not alone at Ephesus, but almost throughout all Asia, this Paul hath persuaded and turned away much people, saying that they be no gods, which are made with hands" (19:24-26).

19. They learned to *hold steady in an uproar:* "And after the uproar was ceased, Paul called unto him the disciples, and embraced them, and departed for to go into Macedonia" (20:1).

Wesley focused his concern for scriptural Christianity on the fullness of the Holy Spirit. And so may we. The Holy Spirit is not a quick fix or a spiritual laser beam that brings off bloodless surgery on passive souls. The Holy Spirit is the active Agent of God who dwells fully in the lives of those Christians who will receive Him. In cooperation with the human nature of man, the Holy Spirit became the plus factor, the Resource, the Generator of power, purity, and purpose in living.

II

THE THERAPY OF
THE SPIRIT

Chapter 8

Overcoming Separation and Loneliness

The saddest fact about man's predicament is his alienation. Separation and loneliness are a dread at any age. The worst punishment a prisoner can be given is total isolation, when time loses its value and contacts with the real world are reduced to a food tray under the door twice a day. Even day and night in isolation cells get blurred into one indistinguishable line. The worst punishment for a child is not a spanking, but separation from the other children and the flow of activity in the home, spending time behind a closed door, separated from everyone else. No teenager can feel a heavier hand of discipline than to be grounded without wheels and restricted from use of the telephone. And none of us ever hurts more than when we feel totally isolated, when no one knows and no one cares.

However, the depressing phenomenon of the times is the great proportion of people today in every culture who are experiencing all of the negative factors in alienation, isolation, and separation while surrounded by crowds of disinterested people. The Chinese call this isolation living death. And in their culture they produce this living death as a means of punishment by acting like a person is dead and therefore pretending not to see or hear him.

There are several reasons why people are lonely. (1) Some people are shy and withdrawn from life because they are afraid of being hurt when they trust anyone. The hurt they got in some past relationship makes them afraid to be vulnerable again in a fulfilling friendship. (2) Others are alienated because someone taught them in childhood they were not a worthwhile, valuable person. They are alienated by their own feelings of inadequacy. (3) Still others feel lonely and alienated from life because they have lost someone or something that leaves their life incomplete. (4) Finally, some people are alienated and lonely because of sins they fear may be uncovered if they open up to people.

In all these cases the result is the same. Dominated by feelings of separation and alienation, thought patterns and relationships develop into attitudes and life-styles that only serve to complicate our existence. These negative feelings feed on themselves and become self-fulfilling prophecies on events and circumstances designed to frustrate our personal growth and development. We spite ourselves by further alienation through attitudes that make it hard for people to like us and by conduct that is guaranteed to keep most people at a safe distance.

Unless God is given a chance to break this self-defeating cycle of negativism, it enlarges itself, feeds on itself, and increases the consequences of its own destructive forces.

God's process for breaking the self-defeating cycle of sin is twofold. *First,* there is forgiveness and restoration. Regeneration makes possible a new beginning. This is God's act of redemption, which restores a person to a new beginning through a new life in Christ. And *second,* there is the sanctifying grace of God that enables us to fulfill the promise of the new beginning. Man is not only saved from sin but also saved to a new set of relationships founded on love of God, love of others, and self-acceptance.

General William Booth of the Salvation Army recruited his converts from the social sewers that ran through the drinking houses and slums of East London. There the civil rejects reinforced their personal sense of negative worth from interaction with each other as they joined together in the public houses seeking escape through the bottle. Advertising over the doors of the saloons was forlorn: "Drunk for a penny, dead drunk for two pennies, and clean straw for three cents."

Booth had a threefold program: (1) He believed in an instantaneous conversion. (2) He believed every converted sinner should be out on the streets the next day, telling about his new life. Therefore he gave his converts a drum to beat, a tambourine to shake, and a street meeting where they could testify. In fact, Booth wanted new converts to witness in front of the same pubs where they drank, telling their conversion experience to their friends. And (3) He wanted all his converts to go forward into holiness. He saw the sanctifying grace of God as the stabilizing force in their lives.

There are four New Testament ideas about the sanctifying grace of God for believers. Although these four ideas are woven into the fabric of the Scriptures, they may be summarized in statements by John, the closest friend of Jesus; by Paul, who was Christ's greatest apostle; and by the writer of Hebrews.

The Promise

A Scriptural Stepping-stone . . .

Although John lived to the ripe old age of more than 90 years, he was just a young man in Jerusalem on the night before the Crucifixion when he heard what Jesus said about the Holy Spirit, whom Christ called the Comforter.

> If ye love me, *keep my commandments.* And I will pray the Father, and he *shall give you another Comforter,* that he may *abide with you for ever;* even the Spirit of truth; whom the *world cannot receive,* because it seeth him not, neither knoweth him: but ye know him; for he dwelleth with you, and shall be in you. *I will not leave you comfortless:* I will come to you.
>
> John 14:15-18

*   *   *

One fact is clear in this paragraph from Jesus' discussion with His disciples on the night of His arrest. He promised the Holy Spirit in a way unknown before in the ancient world. The Holy Spirit had anointed the heroes of ancient Israel for achieving mighty acts of valor. But now Jesus was promising the Holy Spirit as a living presence. (1) The Spirit will only come to those who love Christ and are obedient to Him. (2) The Comforter, who is the Holy Spirit, is the abiding presence of Christ, the risen Lord. (3) The world cannot receive the Holy Spirit. (4) The Holy Spirit is a presence or a person just as Jesus was a person. The Holy Spirit, who comes to fulfill

78

our lives, is not a theology. He is not an experience. He is a person, the adorable Third Person of the Trinity.

The Pattern

A Scriptural Stepping-stone . . .

Paul, who was Christ's greatest apostle, had a clear understanding of the Holy Spirit and His work in believers: *"Husbands, love your wives,* even as *Christ also loved the church,* and *gave* himself for it; that he might *sanctify* and *cleanse* it with the washing of water by the word, that he might present it to himself a glorious church, *not having spot,* or *wrinkle,* or any such thing; but that it should be *holy and without blemish"* (Eph. 5:25-27).

* * *

Many scholars believe Paul was married during his younger years, because he was a member of the Sanhedrin, which required marriage for membership. But even if he were married in his youth, Paul lived out his entire ministry as a bachelor, seeing life through the eyes of a single person. Nonetheless, he had divine inspiration when he saw the pattern of marriage in the work of the Holy Spirit.

The best analogy Paul could give on how the Holy Spirit works in fulfilling lives is the illustration of a man deeply in love with a wife who is fully committed to him. In this life, the best antidote to loneliness, alienation, and separation is a good marriage. (1) Marriage is based on a sacrificial love. Husbands and wives in a good marriage are scarcely aware of their sacrifices for each other because these come naturally

79

from unconditional love. (2) Love is a cleansing experience. And (3) Love is a glorious relationship. This analogy of married love is a beautiful picture of the two-way love there is in God's sanctifying grace. By His grace the dread spirit of alienation and loneliness is replaced with a love that gives and forgives.

The Provision

A Scriptural Stepping-stone . . .

The unknown writer to the Hebrews was never hesitant to write about peace and perfection: "Now the God of *peace,* . . . make you *perfect* in every good work to do his will, working in you that which is wellpleasing in his sight, through Jesus Christ" (Heb. 13:20-21).

* * *

There is only one Source for sanctifying grace, and that is God himself. If God is able to save, He is able to keep. If He is able to forgive, He is able to cleanse. If He is able to save, He is able to sanctify.

God's sanctifying grace is a fulfilling grace. Christian perfection is the fulfillment of all God ever intended us to be. We may not be perfect in performance, but we can be perfectly molded to God's intention. J. Wilbur Chapman once asked General Booth how he had been able to do so much for God. He replied, "I gave God all there was of William Booth." When this happens, God will "make you perfect . . . to do his will, working in you that which is wellpleasing in his sight" (Heb. 13:21).

Chapter 9

Healing the Mind

Scriptural Stepping-stones

Wash me . . .

> *Have mercy upon me, O God, . . . blot out my transgressions. Wash me throughly* from mine iniquity, and *cleanse me* from my sin. For *I acknowledge my transgressions:* and my sin is ever before me. *Against thee, thee only have I sinned,* . . . Behold, *I was shapen in iniquity;* and in sin did my mother conceive me.
>
> Ps. 51:1-5

* * *

Purge me . . .

> *Purge me with hyssop,* and I shall be clean: *wash me,* and *I shall be whiter than snow.* . . . *Create in me a clean heart, O God; and renew a right spirit within me.*
>
> Ps. 51:7, 10

* * *

Restore me . . .

> *Restore unto me the joy* of thy salvation; . . . *Then will I teach transgressors* thy ways; and sinners shall be converted unto thee. . . . *my tongue shall sing aloud* of thy righteousness.
>
> Ps. 51:12-14

Few things, if any, are more tragic than the adulterous breakdown of a man who is respected for his goodness. This was the case with King David. A rock from his sling slew Goliath. The music from his harp calmed the nerves of an anxious king. He knew the solidarity of a loyal relationship with Jonathan. He was a man of mercy who restrained himself from violence when he could have slain his enemy, Saul. And he rode to the accolades of the people who sang his praises in the streets. He was a general who excelled and the king who led Israel to her highest heights in national and international stature.

But David destroyed himself when he allowed a sexually stimulating situation to develop into an adulterous relationship. He seduced Bathsheba and had a child by her. Then he became an accessory to the murder of her husband to cover up his first sin. He sent her husband into battle and then withdrew the troops from about him so Uriah, her husband, was sure to be killed. And then David became victim of the ultimate sin of indifference to all he had done. He tried to go on living as though nothing had ever happened (2 Samuel 11—12).

At the most unsuspecting time, when David thought he had put it all behind him and had successfully rationalized all he had done, the prophet Nathan entered the picture. He told King David a parable about a rich and powerful man who had many sheep but took a ewe lamb by force from a poor neighbor. David responded to Nathan with self-righteous anger, demanding to know the name of the offender so he could correct the injustice to the poor man and punish the rich man who was a guilty thief. David, however, was not ready for Nathan's direct response—"Thou art the man" (2 Sam. 12:7).

With a long, accusing finger and a voice lifted in outrage and conviction, Nathan nailed David to the wall like a javelin thrown by an elite member of the king's bodyguard.

The prophet Nathan was God's messenger for bringing David to his senses. The king had come a long way since his days as an innocent, naive shepherd boy. But the rules of God still applied to him, and his own moral nature was outraged. His soul was stricken with guilt, self-rejection, hurt, sense of sin, and confusion. He needed the cure of the mind that God alone could give. And David was ready for it.

The 51st psalm is David's prayer for restoration and cleansing. The contents of these supplications are almost too personal to watch. Through this psalm we look through a drawn curtain at a most private situation as a man struggles with the outrage of his own conscience. The psalm is divided into four sections: (1) the call, (2) the confession, (3) the cure, and (4) the commitment.

The Call for Mercy

A Scriptural Stepping-stone . . .

Have mercy upon me, O God, according to thy lovingkindness: according unto the multitude of thy tender mercies *blot out* my transgressions. *Wash me* throughly from mine iniquity, and *cleanse* me from my sin.

Ps. 51:1-2

*   *   *

David used three words to describe his miserable condition. Each word, though somewhat synonymous, has its own special meaning. The words "blot," "wash," and "cleanse" are used interchangeably like fever, infection, and sickness are often used to describe the same condition; yet each word has its own meaning. So David used these words to describe his predicament. (1) Transgressions: This is willful disobedience, the behavior of a man who knew better. (2) Iniquity: This idea of iniquity describes the condition and sense of guilt. And (3) Sin: Sin is the sum of the attitudes and actions that fall short of God's behavior norms. All of these words—"transgressions," "iniquity," "sin"—are ways of describing the soul that needs the therapy that only God can give.

David used three words in calling for God's mercy. (1) "Blot out my transgressions": David calls for God to clear the record of his heinous trespasses. (2) "Wash me throughly": The filth of his soul needed to be washed away, the guilt obliterated. (3) "Cleanse me": This is the action of God's mercy, which takes away the condition of sin as the smelter takes away the dross from the ore and leaves pure gold.

In his call for mercy there is one petition David could not make. He could not ask God to remove the consequences of his sin. The baby was still born out of wedlock. The husband of Bathsheba was still in the grave. And the memory of what he had done was etched eternally on the wall of David's mind. God can cure the soul, but even He cannot remove the consequences.

I Am Wrong

A Scriptural Stepping-stone . . .

> For *I acknowledge my transgressions:* and *my sin is ever before me.* Against thee, thee only, have *I sinned,* and done this evil in thy sight: that thou mightest be justified when thou speakest, and be clear when thou judgest. Behold, *I was shapen in iniquity;* and in sin did my mother conceive *me.*
>
> Ps. 51:3-5

*   *   *

My youngest son startled me the other day when he declared, "Dad, you can't ever change for the better until you are willing to say, 'I have a problem and it's my fault.'" Until we are willing to acknowledge our personal responsibility for our predicament, we only project the reasons for our hurt on other people. This projection increases the degree of our hurt and reduces the possibility of a cure. David is a classic example of a man who was willing to admit, "I am wrong."

Fourteen times in five verses David used the personal pronouns that identify his own responsibility. "I acknowledge my transgressions." There is no soul cure for the person who refuses to acknowledge personal responsibility for sin. There is a certain appreciation for David since he did not try to blame Bathsheba, or say everybody's doing it, or say it was the fault of his glands. David accepted his own personal responsibility. He acknowledged responsibility for his own bad conscience. "My sin is ever before me." And he acknowledged the sinful bent of his own nature. "I was shapen in iniquity."

The Cure of the Soul

A Scriptural Stepping-stone . . .

Behold, thou desirest truth in the inward parts: and in the hidden part thou shalt make me to know wisdom. *Purge* me with hyssop, and I shall be clean: *wash* me, and I shall be whiter than snow. Make me to hear joy and gladness . . . *Create* in me a clean heart, O God; and *renew* a right spirit within me. . . . *Restore* unto me the joy of thy salvation; and *uphold* me with thy free spirit.

Ps. 51:6-8, 10, 12

*   *   *

David knew the cure had to be from the inside out—"the inward parts." In this segment of his prayer David uses three strong verbs to describe how God's mercy works in healing the inner mind: (1) "Purge me": Hyssop was used in the ceremonial purification of persons healed of leprosy (Lev. 14:1-9). God can purge the pollution of the soul, removing the dirt and leaving the inner man "whiter than show" and with a new song of "joy and gladness." (2) "Create in me": This is the verb used in the opening sentence of the Bible, "In the beginning God created . . ." (Gen. 1:1). The God who can create the world and make man from its dust is able to do a new creation within the human heart that has been soiled through misuse. (3) "Restore me": The salvation God restores is a joyous fellowship with himself. He gives His people a new spirit and a willing spirit that replaces the bent toward sinning. He implants a disposition that feeds on doing God's will and keeping His law.

The Commitment

A Scriptural Stepping-stone . . .

Then *will I teach* transgressors thy ways; and sinners shall be converted unto thee. Deliver me from bloodguiltiness, O God, thou God of my salvation: and *my tongue shall sing* aloud of thy righteousness.

Ps. 51:13-14

* * *

When God cures the sin-sick soul and restores man to a new set of relationships, David and all the sons of man since his day acknowledge a new responsibility to be a living witness to the healing. Recently I met a man who had been healed of cancer some years ago. No one had to urge him to tell his story. His abounding joy could not be contained. And so it is with the cure of the soul. David promised God he would do two things: (1) "I will teach" and (2) "my tongue shall sing." The most effective teaching comes out of personal experience. And there is no song like the inner melody of a soul set free.

Chapter *10*

A Prayer for Stability

Nothing reveals the character of a Christian leader more than his prayers. When we have forgotten many things about the leaders we have known and loved, we can often recall their prayers.

The most remembered words Jesus uttered on earth are a prayer. Catholics, Protestants, liberals, conservatives, and Eastern Orthodox worshipers can all unite in repeating the Lord's Prayer. Albert Hay Malotte's musical version of our Lord's prayer has inspired people in a wide variety of places, from wedding chapels to music halls.

Nothing tells us more about the heart of Moses than the intercessory prayer he made for his people who had failed him and had forgotten God when they made a golden calf for worship. Returning to the mountains, his heart fell open for us to see his passionate love for the people who reluctantly followed him into the desert and now struck their deepest blow of insurgence in their orgy before a home-crafted animal they had made into an idol. Hear the pathos in Moses' voice which is the agony of his heart turned into words: "if thou wilt forgive their sin—; and if not, blot me, I pray thee, out of thy book which thou hast written" (Exod. 32:32).

The heart of King David is laid open wide in the prayer he made in sorrow for the devastating sequence of events involved in his adultery with Bathsheba. He has the mind of repentance and contrition when he prays, "Have mercy upon me, O God, . . . For I acknowledge my transgressions: and my sin is ever before me. . . . Restore unto me the joy of thy salvation" (Ps. 51:1, 3, 12).

A near rival to the Lord's Prayer is the prayer Jesus made for His enemies. There is nothing but unconditional forgiveness for the men who had hurt Him most: "Father, forgive them; for they know not what they do" (Luke 23:34).

One of the greatest prayers Paul made was first uttered for the church in Colossae and included in a letter he wrote them from his prison cell in Rome. There were reasons for Paul's prayer then that also apply to us now. (1) From their faithful minister, Epaphras, he had learned about their "love in the Spirit" (Col. 1:8). (2) He had heard about the fruit of the Spirit that was beginning to develop in them. And (3) He had heard about the Gnostic heresy being sown among the church members in Colossae that was reducing the suffering of Jesus to a fantasy.

This heresy still appears in the church today among those who want to make Jesus less than the unique God-man. "For this cause" (Col. 1:9), or, "for these reasons," Paul persistently prayed a specific prayer for the people of Colossae. His prayer for them and for us is concerned with matters of Christian growth and stability contained in five petitions. We can only hope that Paul's prayer will be answered in our lives now as it was in the first-generation Christians who lived in what is now South Central Turkey.

*   *   *

A Scriptural Stepping-stone . . .

> For this cause we . . . desire that ye might be filled
> with *the knowledge of his will in all wisdom and
> spiritual understanding;* that ye might *walk worthy
> of the Lord* unto all pleasing, being *fruitful in every
> good work,* and *increasing in the knowledge of God;*
> . . . If ye continue in the faith *grounded and settled,*
> and be not moved away from the hope of the gospel.

> Col. 1:9-10, 23

The Paralysis of Indecision

It is possible to be paralyzed by indecision. There are psychotics in mental hospitals who stand by a chair for two hours, trying to decide whether or not to sit down; or they stand all morning by a closed door, trying to generate enough courage to open it, afraid of what may be on the other side. And many a churchgoer spends much more time fretting over decisions than they do thinking, praying, reading their Bible, and deciding. One of the evidences of maturity is the ability to make a decision and accept its consequences without flinching.

Two key words in this petition related directly to finding God's will are "wisdom" and "understanding." Paul knew that good decisions flow out of "the knowledge of his will in all wisdom and spiritual understanding" (Col. 1:9). (1) There is no substitute for wisdom in making good decisions. Judgment is the flow of psychic energy from which we make the decisions that dominate our lives. This judgment, or flow of decisions, can be either sound or faulty. Good judgment is based on wisdom, which is the application of the knowledge or facts about a problem to the actual decision to be made. This wisdom comes from the discipline of the mind in sorting out the facts in the case. God has blessed us with intellect and experience, which combine in wisdom. (2) Equally important with wisdom is spiritual understanding. The basic principles of biblical law are the beginning of spiritual understanding. There is no ethical way to do an unethical thing, and a closed door may be as much God's will as an open door. Mature Christians have learned how to make decisions based on the common sense of sound judgment and wisdom further enlightened by the voice of God through the Scriptures and the intuitions of the Holy Spirit.

Human Motives

A Scriptural Stepping-stone . . .

That ye might walk worthy of the Lord unto all pleasing, being fruitful in every good work, and increasing in the knowledge of God.

Col. 1:10

*   *   *

Because of the frailties in human nature, such as poor memory, faulty understanding, and inaccurate communicating, it is impossible to be 100 percent consistent in the eyes of everyone. But in his heart of hearts, the mature Christian knows when he has done his best to please the Lord in any given situation, always reaching for the ideal of full consistency with Christian faith.

It is a relief to notice that Paul prayed for a walk "worthy of the Lord unto all pleasing" (Col. 1:10). Only God knows our hearts. He measures our motives, not our movements. It is possible to walk consistently in the eyes of the Lord, because He is pleased with such matters as motivation, intent, direction, and purpose; while the world seldom gives us the benefit of the doubt in these matters. They impugn our motives, discount our intentions, and distort our direction. But mature Christians, nonetheless, never drop the ideal of a consistent life even under the severe scrutiny of our detractors.

Watching the Bottom Line

Paul lived long before businessmen and accountants talked about the bottom line in a commercial enterprise. But Paul had his own way of calling for results in the Christian life. He called on Christians to be "fruitful in every good work" (Col. 1:10). Every Palestinian knew the difference between good fruit and bad fruit and trees with no fruit at all.

Translated into the modern expectations of Christians, there are several characteristics of fruitful Christian service that demand our attention. (1) Dependable follow-through is the beginning of Christian wisdom. A decision to accept Christ is like crossing the border into the Promised Land, while follow-through is the ability to live on the advantages and opportunities the land affords. (2) An understanding of what is to be done is the Christian's job description for service. (3) And there can be no service without sufficient commitment of time and energy to get a job done. (4) Christian service is done to the glory of God, and not for the personal satisfaction of an ego trip. When the total life is lived in service

93

to God, the Christian enjoys the marvelous fruits of fulfillment.

Knowing God Better

Paul's concern for growing Christians was not increased knowledge about God but knowledge based on personal experience with God, "increasing in the knowledge of God" (Col. 1:10). Anyone who wants to spend the time can learn about the president of the United States (1) by hearing others tell about their experiences with him; (2) by reading the best available books about him; (3) by looking at him from a distance, in photographs, or on television; and (4) by hearing his voice as he speaks to others or as he speaks generally to all people.

However, some people do not need to be satisfied learning *about* the president because they *know* him as a personal friend. Although those who know the president personally are by circumstances limited to a fortunate few, it is possible for everyone to know God personally.

The Stretch for Maturity

A Scriptural Stepping-stone . . .

If ye continue in the faith grounded and settled, and be not moved away from the hope of the gospel, which ye have heard, and which was preached to every creature which is under heaven; whereof I Paul am made a minister.

Col. 1:23

*   *   *

Paul mentions three areas of maturity that do not come naturally to man. They are the results of being "grounded and settled." The Christian who has become grounded and settled finds it is easier to be patient, to be long-suffering concerning the failures of others, and to be joyous in spite of the tough circumstances of life's inevitable disappointments. The ill winds of temptation have little effect on Christians who are grounded and settled, for they will not be "moved away from the hope of the gospel."

In all of our daily interactions with people, we are continually generating gratitude or hostility from others. And in all our responses to life, we are becoming more aware of people or more insensitive. Paul's desire was for Christians to be fully mature in both generating gratitude from others by the way we come across to them, and by giving gratitude for life. It is great to be fulfilled.

Chapter 11

The Battle for Your Mind

The greatest battles have not been fought on the beaches of Normandy or in the rice paddies of Southeast Asia, but in the human mind. Your mind is not only the greatest battlefield of your life but also the greatest, most powerful weapon you hold in the high stakes for a fulfilled life. The weak mind that has lost the battle for good thoughts and powerful ideas has settled for a life that suffers from atrophy, boredom, and limited usefulness; while the strong mind wins against the onslaught of pettiness, jaundiced thoughts, and self-centered judgments. The fulfilled life begins in the mind.

The ancient writer of Proverbs declared that a man sooner or later becomes what he thinks: "For as he *thinketh* in his heart, so is he" (Prov. 23:7).

Long before modern studies on human nature determined that peace was in the mind and not in circumstances, the prophet Isaiah wrote, "Thou wilt keep him in perfect peace, whose *mind* is stayed on thee: because he trusteth in thee" (Isa. 26:3).

When Jesus was asked to identify the highest spiritual good, He made it clear that the center of man's relationship with God is in the inner self and not in devotional acts and deeds of goodness: "And thou shalt love the Lord thy God with all thy *heart,* and with all thy *soul,* and with all thy *mind,* and with all thy strength: this is the first commandment"

(Mark 12:30). Paul also made it clear that the remedy for an unfulfilled life is in the mind: "And be not conformed to this world: but be ye transformed by the renewing of your *mind,* that ye may prove what is that good, and acceptable, and perfect, will of God" (Rom. 12:2).

John Wesley must have caught this idea of the mind as Satan's battleground when he wrote, "I would as soon put out my eyes as to lay aside my reason" (*Works,* 4:118). At another time he wrote, "I am ready to give up every opinion which I cannot by calm, clear, reason defend" (*Works,* 5:437).

* * *

A Scriptural Stepping-stone . . .

It is not surprising that James, identified by many as the brother of our Lord, saw the mind as the place and the weapon for all major battles. "My brethren, *count it all joy* when ye fall into divers temptations; knowing this, that the *trying of your faith worketh patience.* . . . If any of you lack *wisdom,* let him ask of God, that giveth to all men liberally, and upbraideth not; and it shall be given him. But let him ask in *faith, nothing wavering.* For he that wavereth is like a wave of the sea driven with the wind and tossed. . . . *A double minded man is unstable* in all his ways. . . . Blessed is *the man that endureth temptation:* for when he is tried, he shall receive the crown of life . . . But *every man is tempted, when he is drawn away of his own lust, and enticed.* Then when lust hath conceived, it bringeth forth sin: and sin, when it is finished, bringeth forth death" (James 1:2-3, 5-6, 8, 12, 14-15).

Tough Times

There are two observations to make on the role of pressures and frustrations in Christian living. First, there is no help for any of us until we accept the problems and trials of life as normal. The most frustrated driver is the one who expects all the other drivers to do properly. Erratic drivers are a part of the hazard of being on the highway. It's a risk to leave home.

And second, there is with every trial the option of joy. Happiness is a choice and not a circumstance. That's why Christians can see joy, challenge, and meaning in their tough times. In fact, there is no maturity without trials. The immature college freshman who causes himself and others trouble is the one whose parents sheltered him from the hurts and disappointments of life. He expects his road to be smooth and for all his friends to run interference for him. And he's frustrated when they don't. The Christian who has learned to accept the inevitability of problems as normal, but opts for joy anyhow, is well along on the royal road to fulfillment.

The Immature Mind

James outlines the four factors usually present in Christians who are the victims of their own immaturity: (1) In the life of every immature Christian there is the *lack of wisdom,* which is just a low level of good common sense. (2) In the life of every immature Christian there is a *wavering faith,* driven about by every wind of disappointment. Always knee-deep in rumors, the wavering Christian is often anxious and afraid. (3) In the life of every immature Christian there is too much dependence on some miracle that is to make up for all the lack of good judgment and wavering faith. And (4) In the life of every immature Christian there is the problem of instability. Immature people quit easily, get discouraged over lack of approval from others, and often live two lives, one at church and the other in the world. Double-mindedness renders the would-be Christian useless to God, to himself, and certainly to anyone else.

The Compensations of Maturity

There are rewards for those who do become mature in dealing with tough times. (1) Mature people are more happy than immature people: "Blessed [happy] is the man that endureth temptation" (James 1:12). (2) Mature people achieve a higher level of self-actualization than immature people: "for . . . he shall receive the crown of life." A fulfilled life itself is the reward of the mature person. (3) Mature people enjoy more of the promises of God. Their will to believe renders its own compensations.

Temptation and Sin

There is a human tendency to blame our problems on someone else, a process psychologists call "projection." But James guides us away from blaming God for our predicament. It is a cop-out to say that it is all right to overindulge our appetites because this is the way God made us. It is a cop-out to say it is His fault, not ours, that we have these urges that lead to sin.

Temptation is generated in circumstances, while sin develops in the will. Temptation to cheat on an income tax report is generated when the circumstances arise that make cheating possible at low risk. But the temptation to cheat never becomes sin until the will receives the signal from the mind to cooperate with the circumstances.

There is an inevitable sequence of (1) temptation, (2) lust, (3) sin, and (4) death: "But every man is tempted, when he is drawn away of his own lust, and enticed. Then when lust hath conceived, it bringeth forth sin: and sin, when it is finished, bringeth forth death" (James 1:14-15). The final consequences of signaling the will to cooperate with the tempting circumstances are sin and death.

Chapter 12

The Seven Big Ifs

Scriptural Stepping-stones

If we say . . .

> *If we say* that we have fellowship with him, and walk in darkness, we lie, and do not the truth: but *if we walk* in the light, as he is in the light, we have fellowship one with another, and the blood of Jesus Christ his Son cleanseth us from all sin. *If we say* that we have no sin, we deceive ourselves, and the truth is not in us. *If we confess* our sins, he is faithful and just to forgive us our sins, and to cleanse us from all unrighteousness. *If we say* that we have not sinned, we make him a liar, and his word is not in us. . . . And *if any man sin,* we have an advocate with the Father, Jesus Christ the righteous . . . And hereby we do know that we know him, *if we keep his commandments.*
>
> 1 John 1:6-10; 2:1, 3

*　*　*

If we walk . . .

> *But if we walk in the light, as he is in the light, we have fellowship one with another, and the blood of Jesus Christ his Son cleanseth us from all sin.*
>
> 1 John 1:7

*　*　*

If we say . . .

> *If we say that we have no sin, we deceive ourselves, and the truth is not in us.*

> 1 John 1:8

* * *

If we confess . . .

> *If we confess our sins, he is faithful and just to forgive us our sins, and to cleanse us from all unrighteousness.*

> 1 John 1:9

* * *

If we say . . .

> *If we say that we have not sinned, we make him a liar, and his word is not in us.*

> 1 John 1:10

* * *

If any man sin . . .

> *And if any man sin, we have an advocate with the Father, Jesus Christ the righteous: And he is the propitiation for our sins: and not for ours only, but also for the sins of the whole world.*

> 1 John 2:1b-2

* * *

If we keep . . .

> *And hereby we do know that we know him, if we keep his commandments.*

> 1 John 2:3

The message John heard about God from Christ was twofold. First, "God is light" (1 John 1:5). This tells us several things about God. (1) If God is light, then He is the essence of all splendor and glory. (2) If God is light, then He speaks to us of white purity and stain-free holiness. (3) If God is light, then He is the Source of illumination for all decisions in life. (4) If God is light, then He is the means for revealing all our flaws and stains. (5) If God is light, then He is eternal. Since all the darkness in the world cannot put out the light of one candle, it is reassuring to know God is the Source of all the light we need for a fulfilled life.

Second, darkness represents all that is hostile to God. This is self-evident truth. Events that promote human debauchery are usually scheduled at night. According to a Boston crime task force, the best single deterrent to thieves who would enter your house is a generous amount of light. "Sunshine laws," open sessions of meetings of governmental agencies, and the very process of courtroom procedures are designed to shed light, illuminate truth, and uncover evil. But in God, there "is no darkness at all" (1 John 1:5).

And third, it is God's plan and purpose for human beings as persons and families and nations to live and walk in fellowship with Him. God is open to us like a great source of light in which there are no threatening shadows or dark places. However, if we would live and walk in fellowship with Him, John mentions seven big "ifs" that must be taken seriously.

Honesty

There is the big "if" of honesty. *"If we say* that we have fellowship with him, and *walk in darkness, we lie,* and do not the truth" (1 John 1:6). (1) There is never any abiding fellowship with each other or with Him until there is abiding honesty. One lie that light reveals will tarnish and often break a friendship. (2) It is possible to be a churchgoing Christian and be living a lie because we "do not the truth" (1 John 1:6). Honesty is not an abstraction, it is visual and concrete. Honesty is a way of life, and there cannot be any fellowship with God without it.

Walking

There is the big "if" of our willingness to walk: "But *if we walk* in the light, as he is in the light, we have fellowship one with another, and the blood of Jesus Christ his Son cleanseth us from all sin" (1 John 1:7). No one can be passive in a relationship without disintegrating it. This is even more true in the relationship with God than it is with people. A Christian cannot be passive in his relationship with God. There are three great ideas here that have to do with us and God: (1) We must "walk in the light." (2) We must "have fellowship one with another." (3) We must be cleansed "from all sin." Failing to walk in the light will distort your vision.

Deceiving

There is the big "if" of indwelling sin: *"If we say* that *we have no sin,* we deceive ourselves, and the truth is not in us"* (1 John 1:8). The Christian who fails to recognize the inner tug-of-war and the spiritual problems that come because of indwelling sin is simply deceiving himself and is not honest with himself and God. Sin as an indwelling presence is not to be confused with sins of the will that result in sinful behavior.

Confessing

There is the big "if" of unrighteousness: *"If we confess our sins, he is faithful and just to forgive us our sins, and to cleanse us from all unrighteousness"* (1 John 1:9).

In God's abounding grace there is process and sequence as well as instantaneous crisis. (1) Salvation begins with confession. Even God cannot help a person who does not want to be helped. (2) Then comes forgiveness. In the new birth, all sins of all kinds are fully forgiven. (3) Then comes cleansing from all sin, the grace of God that sanctifies. (4) And finally, there is a lifetime of growth and development.

Sinning

There is the big "if" of blindness to need: *"If we say* that we have not sinned, we make him a liar, and his word is not in us" (1 John 1:10). There are those who think their personal clout, success, wealth, or power makes them immune to the need for God's forgiveness and cleansing. They ignore sin and even make fun of it. They avoid God by staying away from His house and His people. And as a result, they have no fellowship with Him. They are successful but not fulfilled.

Failing

There is the big "if" of human failure. "My little children, these things write I unto you, that ye *sin not.* And *if any man sin, we have an advocate* with the Father, Jesus Christ the righteous: And he is the propitiation for our sins: and not for ours only, but also for the sins of the whole world" (1 John 2:1-2).

God intends for Christians to live above sin by the cleansing of sin from the will and by the closeness of a daily walk with Him and His people. However, entire sanctification does not remove us from the human race, and there is still the possibility of failure. If and when this happens, "we have an advocate." Our Advocate does not plead our case by asking God to look the other way and act like our disobedience did not happen. But He is our Helper who comes to our side to lift us up and give us a fresh start.

Obeying

There is the big "if" of the commandments: "And hereby we do know that we know him, *if we keep* his commandments" (1 John 2:3).

Two key phrases in the closing verses of this passage make it clear how the commandments of Christ are kept. (1) "The love of God perfected" (1 John 2:5). In Christ the commandments of God are not laboriously kept, they are fulfilled in love. We do not steal from or lie to others when love is the guiding principle in our relationship. Love fulfills the law. (2) "Walk, even as he walked" (1 John 2:6). We do not love people by avoiding them. Love finds a way to walk with people, to listen and talk with them, and to enjoy being in their presence. And so it is in fellowship with God. We walk with Him, listen and talk with Him, and enjoy being in His presence.

Chapter 13

Fulfilled but Still Human

Scriptural Stepping-stones

There arose a murmuring . . .

> *And in those days, when the number of the disciples was multiplied, there arose a murmuring of the Grecians against the Hebrews, because their widows were neglected in the daily ministration.*

> Acts 6:1

* * *

Stephen, full of faith . . .

> *And Stephen, full of faith and power, did great wonders and miracles among the people.*

> Acts 6:8

> *And they were not able to resist the wisdom and the spirit by which he spake. Then they suborned men, which said, We have heard him speak blasphemous words against Moses, and against God.*

> Acts 6:10-11

* * *

While Peter thought . . . the Spirit said . . .

> *But Peter said, Not so, Lord; for I have never eaten any thing that is common or unclean. And the voice spake unto him again the second time, What God hath cleansed, that call not*

thou common. . . . While Peter thought on the vision, the Spirit said unto him, Behold, three men seek thee. Arise therefore, and get thee down, and go with them, doubting nothing: for I have sent them.

Acts 10:14-15, 19-20

*   *   *

No small dissension . . .

When therefore Paul and Barnabas had no small dissension and disputation with them, they determined that Paul and Barnabas, and certain other of them, should go up to Jerusalem unto the apostles and elders about this question.

Acts 15:2

*   *   *

No difference . . .

And God, which knoweth the hearts, bare them witness, giving them the Holy Ghost, even as he did unto us; and put no difference between us and them, purifying their hearts by faith.

Acts 15:8-9

*   *   *

Trouble not . . .

Wherefore my sentence is, that we trouble not them, which from among the Gentiles are turned to God.

Acts 15:19

The miracle of the Holy Spirit at Pentecost leaves Christians in ceaseless wonder, praying, "Lord, do it again."

After Pentecost the Christians had a new motivation, free from inhibiting fears. Peter, who had been frightened into denying his Lord by the accusations of a teenage servant in the courtyard, suddenly lost his fear and led the 120 disciples out of the Upper Room onto the cobblestone streets of Jerusalem where the whole city came to attention, and as many as 3,000 people were converted to faith in Christ in a day.

After Pentecost there was a spirit of love and unity among the disciples that could not be explained outside of the work of the Holy Spirit. Those first followers had every reason to destroy themselves with mass confusion and disorganization. Among their members were a treasurer who sold out and then destroyed himself, a doubter who was notorious for his negative inflexibility, and a powerful group of three men—Peter, James, and John, the latter two sons of thunder—who could dominate most decisions. However, instead of mutually destroying each other, they became known for their love and purity.

After Pentecost there was a power in these Spirit-filled Christians that could not be explained except by the Holy Spirit. The only explanation the Sanhedrin had for the total lack of fear in Peter and John after their arrest was "that they had been with Jesus" (Acts 4:13). The 120 disciples were fishermen, slaves, tax collectors, and nondescript men and women who knew nothing about the levers of power in the Roman world. The powerful Roman rulers tried to ignore them, persecute them, jail them, and burn them at the stake. But in spite of the thundering legions of Rome and the scorn of her philosophers and the laughter of her politicians, Christianity eventually became the official religion of the Roman world.

It is a glorious story, this narrative about these 120, who through the Holy Spirit, developed an unusual level of power, purity, and love. But they were still human. Their feet of clay are evident in a most casual walk through the Book of Acts.

Ananias and Sapphira, in chapter 5, became devious, sacrificed their integrity for personal advantage, and died tragic deaths.

The new Grecian converts, in chapter 6, murmured against the old, established Jews, and the first church board was elected.

Stephen, who was a man of faith and full of the Holy Ghost, in chapter 7, was not protected from evil and died the hard death by stoning.

In chapter 10, Peter, who preached the sermon when the Holy Spirit fell at Pentecost, was so full of racial prejudice that he could not bring himself to go visit the Italian, Cornelius, until God did a special work in his mind.

In chapter 15, there was division in the Church over the theology of works and grace, which resulted in the first general church conference.

It is no wonder Paul wrote to the Christians in Corinth, "We have this treasure in earthen vessels, that the excellency of the power may be of God, and not of us" (2 Cor. 4:7).

The Self-defeating Cycle

One of the big problems among holiness people is knowing the difference between human nature and carnal nature. I have heard preachers describe some facet of human nature and call it carnal. This error has heaped great guilt on sensitive Christians who gave up their faith to go to an altar to be sanctified wholly again. The trip to the altar relieved the guilt, but it did not change human nature. By the time of the next revival they were feeling guilty again and returned to the altar in a self-defeating cycle of guilt and relief, guilt and relief, which ultimately worked to their spiritual devastation. They either gave up or developed a closed system of "dos" and "don'ts" with an accompanying malignancy called self-righteousness.

On the other hand, I have seen Christians deny the evidence of carnality in their lives by calling it human nature. For instance, destructive, prolonged anger is cultivated in some people and kept alive until it turns to maliciousness. All the while the angry person blames this emotional pattern on national origin, the color of his hair, or his genes. It has become fashionable to blame an angry, vindictive personality on a bad childhood environment. Calling carnality natural and blaming it on the environment or the genes blocks the personality of the beautiful cleansing work of the Holy Spirit. And life cannot be fulfilled.

God's Power and Our Power

There are some things sanctification does not do: (1) Sanctification does not destroy our free will. It is possible to sin and backslide even after we have been sanctified entirely. (2) Sanctification does not place us beyond temptation, for we are still human. (3) The crisis experience of sanctification does not make us mature Christians. (4) Sanctification does not make all Christians see things alike, even theologically.

And sanctification does not save us from the rigors of human suffering.

The human predicament is always intermingled with God's glory. (1) "Troubled . . . yet not distressed" (2 Cor. 4:8). The Christian may be at his wit's end, but he is never without hope. (2) "Perplexed, but not in despair" (2 Cor. 4:8). The Christian is never in a corner where there is no way out. (3) "Persecuted, but not forsaken" (v. 9). The Christian may be in trouble, but he is never abandoned. The Psalmist wrote, "When my father and my mother forsake me, then the Lord will take me up" (Ps. 27:10). This balance between God's power and our power must have prompted Paul to write, "But we have this treasure in earthen vessels, that the excellency of the power may be of God, and not of us" (2 Cor. 4:7).

Chapter 14

Staying the Course

During my years as pastor, I sometimes sat back in the swivel chair with my feet on the desk, closed my eyes, relaxed with my fingers locked behind my head, elbows pointing in opposite directions, and asked myself, "If the apostle Paul were pastoring this church, what would he be doing that I am not?"

Some of the most significant factors in my philosophy of pastoral ministry came through repeating this spiritual exercise. For instance, I determined that Paul would not be ignored and unknown in the city. I believe he would have a family church; that he would never be satisfied to confine his ministry within a church building but would get out where the people were; that he would have a Christ-centered church founded on the Bible.

Then, when I became a college president, I kept up the same spiritual exercise: "If Paul were the president of this college, what would he be doing?" (1) I am sure Paul would have a strong academic program. (2) I am sure he would have a strong, orthodox theology department, because he actually wrote most of the basic theology for the Early Church. And (3) I am sure he would have a good-quality athletic program, because he demonstrated knowledge of the Greek games, which were forerunners of the modern Olympics. This is why

115

Paul could think and write naturally about the Christian way as a long race, urging the runners to stay the course.

However, the best analogy of Christian living and the long race on the full length course is described by the unknown writer of Hebrews:

* * *

A Scriptural Stepping-stone . . .

Wherefore seeing we also are compassed about with so great a cloud of witnesses, let us lay aside every weight, and the sin which doth so easily beset us, and let us run with patience the race that is set before us, looking unto Jesus the author and finisher of our faith.

Heb. 12:1-2

The Race Before Us

The Christian race has a goal, which is to become like Jesus. Christians are not set for the 100-yard dash or even the difficult race with high hurdles. The Christian is no hit-and-run artist, no wayfarer, not even a competitor against his fellowman. The Christian is in the long-distance, cross-country race, running against his own record, forever keeping his eyes on Jesus.

There are several characteristics of the long-distance race that relate to the Christian. (1) The long-distance runner never stops training, not even for a day. (2) The long-distance runner has to pace himself to guarantee finishing the race. (3) The long-distance runner must learn how to refurbish himself

116

with food and water on the run. (4) The long-distance runner can never be successful without a good coach whom he accepts as an authority over his life.

The Heritage of the Runners

In the Christian race we have the inspiration of a great heritage. The image here is of a track within a great stadium where the crowds are looking down on the runners. However, in the Christian race there is a different kind of crowd. These stands, which represent the endless heavens, are filled with ex-runners who have already finished the race.

The "cloud of witnesses" (Heb. 12:1) referred to here generates many images. Christians do believe in the unseen, the Holy Spirit, the guardian angels, and the loving gaze of loved ones gone on. Following the death of his father, a football player came directly from the funeral to play in the game. The coach offered to let him off for the evening, but the young man said no. Then explained, "My father was blind, and he never saw me play; but now that he's gone, he'll be watching, and I'm going to play this game for him." In that "cloud of witnesses" are people who care about us intensely. There's inspiration in our heritage.

Our Personal Handicap

In the Christian race there is a handicap. Every Christian's handicap is equal to the unnecessary weights he carries around plus his own besetting sin. The unnecessary weights plus the besetting sin equals the handicap quotient. Distance runners never get encumbered with things.

A Strategy for Finishing

In the Christian race the strategy is the same for each runner: "let us run with patience the race that is set before us" (Heb. 12:1). The Christian needs (1) patience that can be renewed; (2) patience with himself and his own failures; (3) patience with all the other runners who may get in the way; and (4) patience with the racecourse itself, which in long-distance races is flawed and sometimes threatening.

In the Christian race we have the perfect example in Jesus: "who for the joy that was set before him endured the cross" (Heb. 12:2). Jesus is the final Authority in the Christian race, "the author and finisher." (1) He starts us on our race. (2) He judges the finish. And (3) He is the perfect Example.

In the Christian race there is a cost: "lest ye be wearied and faint in your minds" (Heb. 12:3). It is possible to give up before the finish is reached. It is our minds that grow weary and cause us to faint. This is why Paul exhorted the Romans, "Be ye transformed by the renewing of your mind" (Rom. 12:2).

And in the Christian race there is always discipline: "Despise not thou the chastening of the Lord, nor faint when thou art rebuked of him" (Heb. 12:5). Hardship becomes the discipline of God, and no life can have value without discipline. No father nor any coach would be worthy of his name if he failed in discipline. In the Christian race the runner has several options concerning discipline. (1) He can resent it and give in reluctantly. (2) He can choose to react with defiance or respond with gratitude. (3) He may collapse in self-pity. (4) He may view discipline as punishment and be blind to its good side. Or, (5) The Christian may accept discipline and see how God uses it to improve his capacity for being a Christian.

Chapter *15*

The Grace of Tithing

Scriptural Stepping-stones

Bring the tithes . . .

> *Bring ye all the tithes into the storehouse, that there may be
> meat in mine house, and prove me now herewith, saith the
> Lord of hosts, if I will not open you the windows of heaven,
> and pour you out a blessing, that there shall not be room
> enough to receive it.*
>
> Mal. 3:10

*   *   *

Now, the collection . . .

> *Now concerning the collection . . . Upon the first day of the
> week let every one of you lay by him in store, as God hath
> prospered him, that there be no gatherings when I come.*
>
> 1 Cor. 16:1a, 2

Tithing is one of the most misunderstood words in the
English language. Most people have missed what tithing is all
about. It has been thought to be an unfair, worrisome, bur-
densome scheme thought up by some pious Old Testament
writers and latched on to by modern-day pastors as a way to
get the bills of the church paid. Maybe this overstates the fact,
but even so, some fundamental misunderstandings about
tithing do exist.

119

First of all, the very origin of tithing is misunderstood. Abraham and his nephew Lot were rich ranchers. Their cattle and sheep ranged for many miles in all directions from their home place at Hebron. Contention arose over grazing land. The sheepherders and cowpunchers who worked for Lot became very nasty in their dealings with the herdsmen and cowboys who worked for Abraham. So the two men agreed on a division of the land that gave the well-watered plains of Jordan to the young man, Lot.

However, soon after he moved into his new prosperity, a band of five cattle rustlers who lived beyond Damascus saw an opportunity to steal from Lot. In the fracas that resulted, they not only took the sheep and cattle of Lot, but kidnapped him also.

Abraham organized a posse of 318 men who, under heavy arms, chased the marauders to the Euphrates River beyond Damascus. They rescued Lot and retrieved all the plunder. Coming back into their home territory, Abraham, Lot, and all the riders were met by the priest Melchizedek, who provided them with the substances for a service of thanksgiving. And as recognition of God's blessing upon him, Abraham "gave him tithes of all" (Gen. 14:20). The idea of tithing was then passed on from generation to generation.

Second, tithing continued to be a concern of the early patriarchs until the time of the Exodus. Then Moses on Mount Sinai got a message from God, loud and clear. The tithe was no longer to be merely a voluntary act but a part of the principles of godly living. Here is a record of the commandment God gave to Moses: "And all the tithe of the land . . . is the Lord's: it is holy unto the Lord" (Lev. 27:30).

Throughout their history as a chosen nation under God, the children of Israel were a tithing people. The writer of the Proverbs said, "Honour the Lord with thy substance, and with the firstfruits of all thine increase: so shall thy barns be filled with plenty, and thy presses shall burst out with new wine" (Prov. 3:9-10).

Third, tithing is God's plan for the church and the family. People who travel the wheat country of Kansas, Nebraska, the Dakotas, and the Canadian prairies are often struck with the stark outline of a little country church against the sky.

A man in one of these little country churches was asked to serve as treasurer. His church had been unpainted and weather-beaten for years. At certain times during the storms the roof leaked. The congregation had only a part-time pastor, who also served three other congregations. The people in general were discouraged, and nothing was happening.

This man, who operated the local granary, finally agreed to be treasurer of the church for the new year if the congregation would promise not to call for any accounting of the funds until the entire year was finished. Since they were a small church and knew each other well, everyone agreed.

Only a few months after the new church year had begun, the treasurer began to make suggestions to the board on improvements that could be done on their church with the surplus in the treasury. Shocked that there should be money available, they finally took his word for it that the balance was indeed in the bank.

That year they painted the church and put on a new roof. They put more gravel on the parking lot and built a white fence around the entire compound. They brought in a full-time pastor. And when the report was given at the end of the year, they learned that the church had been generous in its contributions to missions.

Amazed that their small congregation could achieve so much financially in a single year, they pressed this marvelous new treasurer to learn the secret. They were all aghast when he told them that his secret was plain and easy.

He said, "All of you brought your grain at harvesttime to my granary. When I figured up how much I owed each one of you, I just deducted 10 percent for the church and gave you the balance without ever saying anything about the deduction. You lived happily and got along well on the nine-tenths, and God's work in our community has prospered more this year than ever before since we have lived here."

We believe in a praying church, a spiritual church, a calling church, and a loyal church, but the most sure way to transform a church and the people in it is for every wage earner in the congregation to become a tither.

That is why the apostle Paul wrote to the church in Corinth, "Now concerning the collection . . . Upon the first day of the week let every one of you lay by him in store, as God hath prospered him, that there be no gatherings when I come" (1 Cor. 16:1*a*, 2).

Chapter 16

Holiness of Heart and Life

Scriptural Stepping-stones

Gird up your mind . . .

> *Wherefore gird up the loins of your mind, be sober, and hope to the end for the grace that is to be brought unto you at the revelation of Jesus Christ.*

1 Pet. 1:13

✳   ✳   ✳

Not fashioning yourselves . . .

> *As obedient children, not fashioning yourselves according to the former lusts in your ignorance.*

1 Pet. 1:14

✳   ✳   ✳

Holy manner of life . . .

> *But as he which hath called you is holy, so be ye holy in all manner of conversation; because it is written, Be ye holy; for I am holy.*

1 Pet. 1:15-16

References in the New Testament to heart holiness, the baptism or outpouring of the Holy Ghost, sanctification, and entire sanctification are like golden threads that shine through on page after page. Never is there a suggestion that heart holiness is optional, offered like two sizes of motors in a new car, nor an accessory to the new birth, like power steering or fog lights are in an auto. Peter, who preached the sermon at Pentecost, later wrote the first-generation Christians, "Wherefore gird up the loins of your mind . . . not fashioning yourselves according to the former lusts . . . so be ye holy in all manner of conversation; because it is written, Be ye holy; for I am holy" (1 Pet. 1:13-16).

Heart holiness is not even an abnormally high level of spiritual existence for spiritually gifted people like Paul and the writer of Hebrews. Heart holiness is for fishermen, farmers, and folks on the street, not just ministers, mystics, and missionaries. Heart holiness is the normal way of living for God. (1) Holiness of life is a process as well as an instantaneous experience. (2) Holiness of life involves the active participation of the Christian in cooperation with the Holy Spirit on a day-to-day basis. (3) Holiness of life is never fully perfect in human terms, but is perfection of motive and intention. (4) Holiness of life continues to develop over a period of years, while holiness of heart is obtained in an instant.

The farmer works and strives for a good crop by much exertion on his own, including plowing, planting, cultivating, tending, and fertilizing. But ultimately the farmer depends upon the rain and sunshine, which are from God and beyond his control. And so the Christian strives and works for holiness of life through self-discipline, study, and correction. But ultimately the Christian depends on the grace of God for forgiveness, cleansing, and empowerment.

Holiness of heart and holiness of life are a joint venture. The Holy Spirit comes into our lives in a special way in the experience that cleanses the heart that we may become holy in life and conduct. Paul understood this principle when he wrote, "According as he hath chosen us in him . . . that we should be holy and without blame before him in love" (Eph. 1:4).

The Scriptures speak of holiness as follows: "God hath not called us unto uncleanness, but unto holiness" (1 Thess. 4:7). "Unto the church of God which is at Corinth, to them that are sanctified in Christ Jesus, called to be saints, with all that in every place call upon the name of Jesus Christ our Lord, both theirs and ours" (1 Cor. 1:2).

Holiness follows initial salvation like marriage follows a wedding or life follows a birth. On the bottom line holiness is the natural sequence in full salvation: "Follow peace with all men, and holiness, without which no man shall see the Lord" (Heb. 12:14).

The Practical Need for Holiness

Holiness of heart and life are necessary for fellowship with Christ. God does not require a flawless life in order to establish fellowship with Him any more than an earthly friendship is based on social perfection. Our human limitations are evident in both our divine and human patterns of fellowship. It is intention and motive that are most important in fellowship.

Holiness of heart and life are necessary for our own continued spiritual well-being. Christian discipline is necessary for a fulfilled life. When God speaks to us about some weakness in our personality or behavior patterns, we need to listen. In this same chapter and almost in the same breath that the writer of Hebrews uses to talk about pursuing holiness in order to see the Lord, he also talks about Christian discipline in the holy life: "My son, despise not thou the chastening of the Lord, nor faint when thou art rebuked of him: For whom the Lord loveth he chasteneth" (Heb. 12:5-6).

The Linkage Between Holiness and Usefulness

Holiness of heart and life are necessary for effective Christian service. Throughout the Scriptures, holiness is linked with usefulness. After the Holy Spirit came, the 120 disciples departed the Upper Room to become witnesses on the streets of Jerusalem. After the Holy Spirit came on the church in Ephesus, the great revival began. Even the word *Spirit* has before it the word *Holy.* The Spirit that is outpoured is the "Holy" Spirit. The Bible is the "Holy" Bible. And the men who were inspired to write the Bible were "holy" men (2 Pet. 1:21). This linkage between holiness and usefulness is what makes the grieving and quenching of the Spirit dangerous (1 Thess. 5:19).

Holiness of heart and life are necessary for the continuance of our assurance of salvation. This idea of linking holiness of heart and life to continuing salvation is counter to the new popular born-again claim that demands no moral change in life. When the editor of a pornographic magazine can be born again and continue to grind out his pornography, there is something wrong somewhere. The most reliable evidence that we are Christians is a holy life demonstrated in attitudes and relationships. "Every man that hath this hope in him purifieth himself, even as he is pure" (1 John 3:3). "For as many as are led by the Spirit of God, they are the sons of God" (Rom. 8:14). Is there practical holiness in my life day by day? Holiness of heart and life are necessary for Christian fulfillment.

III

THE FULFILLED LIFE
AND THE
TRANSFORMED MIND

Chapter 17

The Transforming Gospel

Scriptural Stepping-stones

I am debtor . . .

> *I am debtor both to the Greeks, and to the Barbarians; both
> to the wise, and to the unwise.*
>
> Rom. 1:14

* * *

I am ready . . .

> *So, as much as in me is, I am ready to preach the gospel to
> you that are at Rome also.*
>
> Rom. 1:15

* * *

I am not ashamed . . .

> *For I am not ashamed of the gospel of Christ: for it is the
> power of God unto salvation to every one that believeth; to
> the Jew first, and also to the Greek.*
>
> Rom. 1:16

* * *

The just shall live . . .

> *For therein is the righteousness of God revealed from faith to
> faith: as it is written, The just shall live by faith.*
>
> Rom. 1:17

Except for the Gospels, the most important book in the New Testament is Paul's letter to the Romans. (1) It is the first theology of the Church. (2) It has been a guidebook to orthodoxy in the Church. (3) It has been a central factor in the great spiritual movements of the Church. In fact, the importance of the Book of Romans is difficult to overestimate.

Among the Early Church fathers, Augustine was the spiritual and intellectual giant, who for 30 years was the dominant voice that stood off heresy and reconciled the philosophy of the day with the facts of faith in Christianity. His two books, *The City of God* and *Confessions,* are still studied by university students.

As a young man, Augustine was wayward and in rebellion against the values and priorities of his Christian mother, Monica. But in Italy, Augustine crossed paths with an intellectually superior pastor whose sermons challenged him. Finally, one afternoon in a garden he heard the voices of children at play chanting a phrase that caused him to take up the scroll at his side. As he unrolled it to read, his eyes fell on a passage from Paul in Romans, "Not in rioting and drunkenness, not in chambering and wantonness, not in strife and envying. But put ye on the Lord Jesus Christ, and make not provision for the flesh, to fulfil the lusts thereof" (Rom. 13:13-14). Through the rest of his life and ministry, Augustine pointed back to the garden and the message of God for him in Romans as the point and time of his conversion.

The bomb that shook the Roman church to its foundations at the end of the Middle Ages was a single line from the first chapter of Paul's letter to the Romans, "The just shall live by faith" (Rom. 1:17). The history of the world was changed by a little monk who nailed a list of 95 discussion questions

130

on the door of the castle church in Wittenberg, hoping other concerned scholars, in town for All Saints Day, would respond. The world was changed because Martin Luther read Romans and believed it.

On Sunday, May 24, 1738, John Wesley attended a service in St. Paul's Cathedral in London. With a heart that hungered for peace, and a mind that yearned for truth, Wesley went, somewhat against his will, to a society meeting in an upstairs room in nearby Aldersgate Street. Here he listened while someone read the preface of Luther's commentary on the Epistle to the Romans.

He later wrote, "About a quarter before nine . . . I felt my heart strangely warmed. I felt I did trust in Christ, Christ alone, for my salvation: And an assurance was given me, that he had taken away my sins, even mine, and saved me from the law of sin and death" (*Wesley's Journal,* 1:103). That moment was the turning point in history that saved England from a bloody revolution and launched the great evangelical revival of the 18th century.

A Letter from Paul

Think, then, what it meant in the Early Church to get a letter from Paul. (1) He was the greatest preacher in the Church. (2) He was the chief theologian of the Church. (3) He was the most experienced missionary in the Church. And (4) He was a prime example of the power of Christ to save a soul and radically change a life. Paul's reputation must surely have preceded his letter since, according to the 24 names mentioned in chapter 16, he knew people in Rome who must have traveled in other places where Paul had ministered. And now, here was a letter from Paul, a slave of Jesus, called and separated, with his mission to proclaim the gospel.

For an Englishman, the greatest city in the world would be London; for a German, Berlin; and for a Frenchman, Paris. If this question on the greatest city were asked in the ancient world around the Mediterranean, people would have responded in unison: Rome!

And here in this leading city, unknown in the halls of Caesar was a little congregation of Christians, meeting in homes, who were the object of Paul's concern. They had a Bible that consisted of only 39 books. There was no sponsoring denomination and no administrative oversight. They were humble people who believed that the Messiah who was promised by Isaiah and others in the Scriptures was this same Jesus whom the Jews rejected and the Romans slew, who was raised up from the dead and, after 40 days of proclaiming the kingdom of God, ascended up to heaven. To this small church of humble believers Paul addressed his letter, which was the first theology of the Church. Paul knew the significance of a church in the capital of the world, and he wanted their faith to be founded on sound understanding.

The Passion of Paul

The zeal and passion of Paul is summarized in three statements he makes about himself and his mission. (1) Paul felt a sense of responsibility: "I am debtor" (Rom. 1:14). He felt a responsibility to proclaim the gospel to all the kinds of people in Rome, both high and low. (2) Paul felt a sense of challenge: "I am ready" (v. 15). He was not overwhelmed by the bigness of Rome nor its importance. (3) Paul felt a sense of enthusiasm: "For I am not ashamed" (v. 16). If he were alive today with a bumper sticker on his car, it probably would read, "Christ Is the Answer."

Chapter 18

The Wrath of God

Scriptural Stepping-stones

The wrath of God . . .

> *For the wrath of God is revealed from heaven against all ungodliness and unrighteousness of men, who hold the truth in unrighteousness.*

Rom. 1:18

* * *

God gave them up . . .

> *God also gave them up to uncleanness . . . God gave them up unto vile affections . . . God gave them over to a reprobate mind . . .*

Rom. 1:24, 26, 28

* * *

Worthy of death . . .

> *Who knowing the judgment of God, that they which commit such things are worthy of death, not only do the same, but have pleasure in them that do them.*

Rom. 1:32

For some readers, the Book of Romans seems difficult and would be much more easily understood if it were written in the language and style of the morning newspaper. But Paul was not a reporter writing a chronicle of events. He was a preacher/theologian interpreting the facts of faith about Christ and His life, death, and resurrection, and what it meant to Christians in Rome.

Also, Paul was not writing for publication. He was sending a letter to some flesh-and-blood people in a ghetto church. While ministering in Corinth, faced with all the problems that tore at that church, he wrote a letter to the Christians in Rome, hoping his instructions would save them from the disasters that plagued Corinth. He dictated a Christian guidebook on the meaning of the gospel. Some have even called Romans the Gospel According to Paul.

The people Paul wrote to in Rome were not monks and nuns. They were flesh-and-blood working people who believed Jesus was the Messiah, raised up from the dead by God the Father. They had no ordained ministry. The four Gospels had not yet been written. It had been little more than 25 years since Jesus had lived on earth. To these early believers, Romans was probably the first piece of strictly Christian literature they had seen. Romans was to be their handbook on Christian faith and life.

So now that Paul's introductory remarks were finished, Paul's secretary adjusted himself in his seat and settled into the assignment of recording the purpose and substance of the letter. Paul began with a phrase that can strike horror to a man's heart, "the wrath of God" (Rom. 1:18). This is a terrifying phrase. When the laws of God in human nature are broken, there are consequences and judgments, not rewards and corrections.

The Old Testament prophets believed this era in history, which is evil, will be followed by an age that is good. They also believed the new age would be ushered in by the Day of the Lord, which is to be a day of terrible retribution and judgment. Then they believed the universe will be remade for God's kingdom, which will ultimately be ushered in.

Paul did not tell these Romans that God sent or would send people to hell for these sins he listed or other sins he did not. He says something even more terrible: "God gave them up." Men abandoned by God will make their own place in hell and pave the approaches with sins that demonstrate increasing insensitivity to God's love. This terrible talk about people abandoned by God is based on two facts:

The first fact is free will. Since God endowed man with a will to choose freely the kind of life and faith that guides him, it is possible to have either a saint like Bud Robinson who yielded himself wholly to God, or a lascivious sinner in the Mafia who has surrendered his whole will to evil.

The second reason men are "given up," by even a loving Heavenly Father, is the reality of spiritual distance. The more a man sins, the easier it is to sin. One of the frightening qualities of sin is its power to beget sin. And every sin pushes a man farther from the voice of God until finally God's voice can hardly be heard at all.

Sin is a lie because it leads the sinner into more depraved and complicating sins with a false promise. And in the end sin ruins life for the sinner and all those who look to him. As the distance from God gets greater, the pull of hell gets stronger, and the binding power of evil becomes more difficult to break.

This desolation of the sinner is not the result of an angry God who cries for retribution like a frustrated ruler seeking vengeance on his enemies. The desolated sinner has chosen evil and fortified his choice with enough spiritual distance to make hell a natural consequence, both in this world and in the world to come.

One's addiction to sin leads to a final fix, and the withdrawal pains are more terrible than the sinner is willing to bear. At this point the sinner can no longer tell the difference between good and evil. He has adjusted to sin like an addict does to his drugs. Hell is now but a matter of time in this world and the world to come.

"Wherefore God also gave them up *to uncleanness* through the lusts of their own hearts . . . For this cause God gave them up *unto vile affections:* for even their women did change the natural use into that which is against nature: and likewise also the men, leaving the natural use of the woman, burned in their lust one toward another; men with men working that which is unseemly . . . God gave them over *to a reprobate mind,* to do those things which are not convenient" (Rom. 1:24, 26-28).

Uncleanness

First, God gave them up to uncleanness. God made man for fellowship. God wanted friendship with persons with whom He might walk and talk. But by choice, people have turned away from God to serve themselves. Finally, as the result of their persistence in self-centeredness, God gives them up to "the lusts of their own hearts."

Second, God gave them up to vile affections. The seriousness and sinfulness of homosexuals and lesbians is that their behavior is the result of what can happen when someone has been given up by God. Going into a relationship "which is against nature" was not theoretical thought with Paul. He was writing about a sin that was well known and widely practiced in the days of the Roman Empire. Cultural factors may contribute to the possibility of homosexuality, like poor food contributes to rickets. But homosexuality is ultimately a sin of the will, which can be both forgiven and cleansed.

Third, God gave them over to a reprobate mind. When men deliberately put God out of their lives, things get out of control and life degenerates. (1) Paul's list of evil thoughts, attitudes, and behavior patterns sounds like a clinical report. (2) This list of sins will soon dominate the mind of a person who tolerates them within himself. (3) Enjoying the sins of others is the ultimate result of a reprobate mind.

Chapter 19

The Judgment of God

Scriptural Stepping-stones

Thou art inexcusable . . .

> *Therefore thou art inexcusable, O man, whosoever thou art that judgest: for wherein thou judgest another, thou condemnest thyself; for thou that judgest doest the same things.*

> Rom. 2:1

* * *

We are sure . . .

> *But we are sure that the judgment of God is according to truth against them which commit such things.*

> Rom. 2:2

* * *

The goodness of God . . .

> *Or despisest thou the riches of his goodness and forbearance and longsuffering; not knowing that the goodness of God leadeth thee to repentance?*

> Rom 2:4

* * *

Wrath against the day of wrath . . .

But after thy hardness and impenitent heart treasurest up unto thyself wrath against the day of wrath and revelation of the righteous judgment of God.

Rom. 2:5

* * *

Render to every man . . .

Who will render to every man according to his deeds. . . . For there is no respect of persons with God.

Rom. 2:6, 11

A national parole officer once told me there are no prisoners in federal penitentiaries who feel they belong there. They all believe they have been wronged by the arresting officer, the attorneys, the judge, a prejudiced jury, or an unfair legal system.

There is a well-known set of excuses people draw on when they are caught. (1) One of the most common is ignorance of the law. People who use this excuse say such things as, "I didn't see the sign." "When did they change the rules?" "I didn't know anything about it." (2) The plea that the ends justify the means is another popular excuse. "I didn't intend to speed; I was late for church." "I sped up to avoid an accident" (as if slowing down might have been fatal). (3) Being out of character is another favorite rationalization. "I don't usually drive fast." "I was concentrating on something else and just forgot about the speedometer." "I haven't had a traffic ticket in 10 years." "I drive this same route to work every day, and nothing like this has ever happened before." (4) And it is always easy to say that everyone is doing it. This is a favorite excuse among persons caught in technical irregularities, such as income tax problems.

(5) A final excuse is some form of rationalization. This takes a number of popular forms: *(a)* Degrees of badness. A young man who stole hams from a restaurant kitchen thought he should be excused because someone had left the door unlocked. "I didn't force the lock," he said, with a pitiful expression as though that nullified the stealing of the hams. *(b)* Rationalizing a different set of ethics for wrongs against a corporation or a bureaucracy. Students who would not steal from another student may steal books from the library and say, "It's not anybody's, and anyhow, I pay tuition." With some people, cheating on taxes is a game because, after all, it's the government.

But Paul's conclusion is that, in the sight of God, every man is guilty of sin, and none is excused for his misdeeds. Typical of Paul's style, he outlined the principles of God's judgment that apply to all of us.

First, we see in others our own weaknesses. The man who thinks everyone else is stealing and lying, and constantly points this out in others, is actually identifying these weaknesses in himself. The person with a critical tongue is the first to point out criticism in others. Jesus explained this principle in the Sermon on the Mount when He asked why we concentrate on the mote that is in our brother's eye and fail to recognize the beam that is in our own eye. This is why He said, "Judge not, that ye be not judged. For with what judgment ye judge, ye shall be judged" (Matt. 7:1-2).

Second, God's judgment is without error. There are several ways to escape punishment in a court of law: (1) There may be lack of evidence. (2) There may be a technicality that makes the judge dismiss the charges. (3) The defendant may jump bail, escape from jail, or possibly never be caught in the first place. But with God there are no errors. God has all the evidence there is. There is no way of escape. He knows all, and there is no place His Spirit cannot go. In God's system of justice there are no cases dismissed on grounds of improper procedure or technical points of law.

Third, God's goodness is designed to lead us to repentance. Paul uses three important words that help explain God's efforts in this regard. (1) *Goodness.* Even though we do not deserve it, God is still kind as He moves to bring us to repentance. (2) *Forbearance.* God does not collect all His debts on the day they are due Him. Although sin has its immediate consequences, the full and final wrath of God is withheld in order that men may have time to repent. (3) *Longsuffering.* God is, by nature, patient with people, even those who deserve it least. When God has the power and the right to avenge himself against those who ignore or reject Him, He is still patient.

Fourth, God's judgment is based on our works. It is impossible to separate life and breathing. Where there is life, there is breath; and where there is breath, there is life. Faith also does not happen in a vacuum. It is not self-contained. Some form of the verbs "do" or "go" is used more than twice as many times as "faith" in the New Testament. Faith issues in works. Out of faith comes the fruit of the Spirit. In an effort to highlight the importance of faith and dependency of salvation on faith, some have tried to downgrade the central importance of Christian works as a demonstration of Christian faith. But salvation does not work that way. Jesus said, "By their fruits ye shall know them" (Matt. 7:20). James said, "Shew me thy faith without thy works, and I will shew thee my faith by my works" (James 2:18).

Fifth, with God all people are equal. In God's international law there is no "favored nation" clause. America is a strong country that specializes in religious liberty and the great humanitarian Christian values of equality, freedom, and the rights of the individual person; but America will reap the consequences of its sin just like Israel, Russia, Germany, or any other nation.

God also has a "no favored person" clause in His judgments on people. Those with much light will be judged against the light they have known; and those with little light, on their minimum exposure to truth. But one thing can be counted on: God's judgments are fair and God's judgments are inescapable.

Chapter 20

Knowing God Better

Men have tried to achieve a right relationship with God by offering Him a sacrifice. In the ancient world people tried this. But sacrifice, unfortunately, became a substitute for obedience and fellowship.

*   *   *

A Scriptural Stepping-stone...

The protest of the prophets against the inadequacy of this idea is summed up in the words of Micah, "Wherewith shall I come before the Lord, and bow myself before the high God? shall I come before him with burnt offerings, with calves of a year old? Will the Lord be pleased with thousands of rams, or with ten thousands of rivers of oil? shall I give my firstborn for my transgression, the fruit of my body for the sin of my soul? He hath shewed thee, O man, what is good; and what doth the Lord require of thee, but to do justly, and to love mercy, and to walk humbly with thy God?" (Mic. 6:6-8).

*   *   *

Men have tried to achieve a right relationship with God by keeping His law meticulously. Jews who were contemporary with Paul, who had not believed on Jesus, did believe that God had set forth His will in His law and that the way to fellowship and being approved with God was to keep His law fully.

There were several problems with this idea of earning God's love by keeping His law. (1) It was impossible to keep the law without flaw, especially the ceremonial law, which covered many details of worship and life. (2) There were many interpretations of the law. For instance, "Remember the sabbath day, to keep it holy" (Exod. 20:8) is a basic concept in the Ten Commandments. But there were as many ideas on how to keep the Sabbath day as there were people to keep it. (3) Almost without fail, people who worked hard at keeping the law became self-righteous about their achievements. This led to conceit and complacency among those who "trusted in themselves that they were righteous, and despised others" (Luke 18:9). Jesus directed His strongest statements against the Pharisees who preached and practiced this way of access to God.

Men have tried to achieve a right relationship with God by their good works. People like Paul worked their way up the ladder of good works to the top only to find their ladder was leaning against the wrong wall. Trying to build credit with God by human works led to despair and not hope. No man is good enough to earn salvation.

These three, (1) inadequacy of the sacrificial lamb, (2) the frustration in trying to keep the law perfectly, and (3) the shortness of the ladder built on good works, all failed because they could not be perfect. Hope was overcome by despair as the verdict always came back, "Guilty!" And it was no special comfort to know the verdict was universal because all men fell short of the glory of God.

148

No one knows how or when Paul broke through the problem with the answer that he saw in Jesus. Some believe his disciplined mind and keen intellect were inspired of God to discover the answer to a right relationship with God during his two years in Arabia just after his conversion and escape over the wall in Damascus. However, the answer that was revealed to him made sense to the Christians in Rome and eventually to the whole Church who got copies of his letter. Paul's explanation was not one man's idea. It was truth in the 1st century and in the 20th century, in Rome and in every city and hamlet on earth. Paul's conclusion was that "a man is justified by faith without the deeds of the law" (Rom. 3:28). God justified man "freely by his grace" (v. 24). To the Christians in Rome this was a radically new idea. For all who believed this gospel, it was Good News.

* * *

A Scriptural Stepping-stone . . .

Being *justified freely by his grace* through the *redemption that is in Christ Jesus:* whom God hath set forth to be *a propitiation through faith* in his blood, to declare *his righteousness for the remission of sins* that are past, through the forbearance of God; to declare, I say, at this time his righteousness: that he might be just, and *the justifier of him which believeth in Jesus.*

Rom. 3:24-26

* * *

149

There are four questions that will help us understand better how we can know God:

What is grace? Since no man can make it on his own, because "all have sinned, and come short of the glory of God" (Rom. 3:23), Paul came to realize that a right relationship with God could be gained only by God's free grace, extended to us as a gift, not because we have earned it but because He loves us.

What is faith? Faith is God's one requirement of us. But faith is not some deed a man does or some virtue he puts into practice. Faith is believing that God accepts me—"Just as I am, without one plea."

How is God's grace connected to the death of Jesus and His resurrection? No one can fully explain how "God was in Christ, reconciling the world unto himself" (2 Cor. 5:19). God did the work for us through Jesus Christ. Jesus, the perfect Fulfillment of all the law, became the ultimate Sacrifice for our sins.

What happens when a person accepts the grace of God through faith "in Christ Jesus"? (1) We are "justified freely." If an innocent man appears before a judge, he is acquitted. But in the case of man before God, all are guilty and without excuse. Yet God, because of Christ, by His grace, treats the believer as if he had never been guilty. (2) Then, by this grace we are saved through Christ Jesus. Man, sold in sin and unable to buy his own freedom, could become free from the slavery of sin "through the redemption that is in Christ Jesus." (3) Finally, Christ was the ultimate Sacrifice, the Propitiation for our sins. By His life of obedience and death, Christ atoned fully for all the sins of all the people in the world, including you and me.

Chapter 21

Justification

In the Bible there are numerous watershed statements. These are truths from which other truth flows. One of these landmark statements is the opening sentence in the Bible: "In the beginning God created the heaven and the earth" (Gen. 1:1). There is no effort to prove the existence of God, tell where He came from, or explain His ultimate purpose. There is just the flat-out fact that in the beginning there was God, and He created what was created. If this fact is accepted as truth, many other Bible facts fall into place and find their meaning. If this truth is rejected, then much of the Bible becomes useless nonsense and makes the biological theory of evolution and the other positions of the agnostics more acceptable.

Another landmark statement is found in the opening verse of the 23rd psalm. The first five words unlock the entire psalm: "The Lord is my shepherd." If this viewpoint is believed, other truths in the psalm flow in natural sequence: (1) "I shall not want"; (2) "He maketh me to lie down in green pastures"; (3) "He leadeth me beside the still waters." These and other truths in the 23rd psalm are subject to our confidence in the opening statement.

Paul's statement on God's love for sinners is one of the most important doctrinal watersheds in the New Testament. "God commendeth his love toward us, in that, while we were yet sinners, Christ died for us" (Rom. 5:8). All of Christian faith rests on this proclamation. There are several thoughts tied together in this broad truth that give meaning and understanding to the concept of justification. (1) The death of Christ is a fact not open for debate. What happened to Christ on a cross planted in a hill north of Jerusalem in the spring, A.D. 30, is an established fact. Jesus is a person, a historical figure who lived and died. (2) Christ not only lived and died but also died "for us." It is not enough to say Christ died. There was purpose in His death; He died to take away our sins, to pay for our pardon. That phrase "for us" adds an altogether new meaning to the death of Jesus. (3) But there is still an additional fact to be considered. The love of God is revealed in the death of Christ for us as sinners who did not deserve His love. "God commendeth his love . . . while we were yet sinners, Christ died for us." So it can be seen that in several interrelated ways, this statement is a most important truth. Because this statement is true (and Paul believed it as a fact of faith), Paul points out five consequences.

*　*　*

A Scriptural Stepping-stone . . .

Much more then, being now *justified by his blood,* we shall be *saved from wrath* through him. For if, when we were enemies, we were *reconciled to God* by the death of his Son, much more, being reconciled, we shall be *saved by his life.* And not only so, but *we also joy* in God through our Lord Jesus Christ, by whom we have now *received the atonement.*

Rom. 5:9-11

*　*　*

First, we are justified by His blood. Because Christ died for us, we are cleared from all guilt for our sins. In a modern court of law, the defendant is justified when convincing evidence is presented proving his behavior did not break the law. But in God's plan, the defendant is justified when his guilt is obvious and admitted. While the guilty person sings, "Just as I am, without one plea," God adjusts the record as though he had never been guilty in the first place.

Second, we shall be saved from wrath. Because Christ died, our punishment is canceled, even for all eternity. After an afternoon of pastoral counseling I have sat exhausted in my swivel chair and said, "If some people had sat down 10 years ago and written across the top of a yellow pad of paper, 'What can I do to get my life into the biggest possible mess in the next 10 years?' they would not have done as well as they have, all because of sin." And those who persist in going against the face of God will suffer the wrath that begins in this world and comes to its full force in the judgment of the world to come. Just as "eternal life" is a quality of life that begins in this world and is ultimately fulfilled in the next, so the wrath of God is operative immediately in this life and will be ultimately fulfilled in the life after the final judgment. But, because "Christ died for us . . . we shall be saved from wrath."

Third, we are reconciled to God. Because Christ died for us, the barriers between God and us are removed. Have you ever been alienated from somebody you loved? Have you ever felt like everything you did to help a bad situation was rejected, and your efforts at goodwill even made the estrangement worse? Then, have you had something wonderful happen that changed everything, bringing you back into fellowship with your alienated friend? All of us are, by nature and conduct, sinners, alienated from God. It was not God who was reconciled at Calvary. It is we sinners who are reconciled to God.

Fourth, we shall be saved. Because Christ died for us, we (1) shall be saved from wrath, (2) were reconciled to God, and (3) now are "saved by his life." The believer is not only saved *from* something but also saved *to* something. We are saved from wrath, and we are saved to eternal life.

Fifth, we have now received the atonement. Because Christ died for us, His sacrifice is operative in our behalf. Salvation, wrath, reconciliation, joy, and atonement—these are strong words that help describe what happens to persons who believe Christ died for us. The central thought in Christian faith as clearly explained by Paul is man's inability to earn or deserve the favor of God. Salvation is shown to be by grace, free and undeserved, the result of God's love for us, even while we were yet sinners. One of the best ideas Paul uses to explain God's grace is atonement, which means to be at one with God.

Chapter 22

Sanctification

The church challenges the minds and hearts of its people to a full life in Christ Jesus, cleansed from sin by the power of His death and resurrection, filled with the presence of the Holy Spirit, and demonstrated in Christian love. This is the goal and reason for the existence of the church. The mission of the church is unique in the proclamation of the possibility and necessity of the fullness of the Holy Spirit in the believer, as indicated in the New Testament, and especially emphasized in Paul's letter to the Romans.

One of the problems many Christians face is the variety of standards preached as evidence of the Holy Spirit in Christian living. The real meaning of the fully sanctified life goes much deeper than mere human behavior, which can be conditioned by psychological processes and controlled through discipline. Sanctification is a heartrending experience of self-emptying and a glorious response to the Holy Spirit as the supreme thrust in one's spiritual life.

The processes that prepare the Christian to receive the experience of entire sanctification are (1) the abdication of self from the throne of one's life in favor of the complete Lordship of Jesus Christ, (2) the consecration of all that one is, and ever hopes to be, to the purposes of God's will, and (3) the commitment of every issue of life beyond human control into the hands and purposes of God. All three of these factors are wrapped up in the mind, emotions, and will.

Justification does not happen of itself. There really is no such thing as receiving God's forgiveness in isolation, of itself, because justification is welded to sanctification. If Paul's letter to the Romans stopped with chapter 4, there would be reason to misunderstand him. But in chapter 6 Paul makes it clear that the Christian is "made free from sin" to become "the servant . . . of righteousness." In the life of the born-again Christian, the Holy Spirit will do a cleansing work, setting him free from his sinful nature. "But now being made free from sin, and become servants to God, ye have your fruit unto holiness, and the end everlasting life" (Rom. 6:22).

* * *

A Scriptural Stepping-stone . . .

Likewise *reckon ye also yourselves to be dead indeed unto sin,* but alive unto God through Jesus Christ our Lord. *Let not sin therefore reign* in your mortal body, that ye should obey it in the lusts thereof. Neither yield ye your members as instruments of unrighteousness unto sin: but *yield yourselves unto God,* as those that are alive from the dead, and your members as instruments of righteousness unto God . . . For *sin shall not have dominion over you:* for ye are not under the law, but under grace. . . . But now *being made free from sin,* and become servants to God, *ye have your fruit unto holiness,* and the end everlasting life.

Rom. 6:11-14, 22

* * *

In sanctification, there is death to sin: "Reckon ye also ... dead indeed unto sin" (Rom. 6:11). Paul used baptism to illustrate the meaning of death to sin and resurrection into a new life. Most of Paul's converts came to Christ directly from a pagan world. Often the new Christian was tearing himself away from his old roots, even from family, and always from old sinful habits. For most of them, serving Christ was a matter of beginning life all over again. As the new Christian felt the baptismal waters close in over his head, it was like being buried, and as the new Christian came out of the water, it was like being raised into a new life. When a Christian has died to sin and been resurrected to a new life in Christ, there is more than legal justification, there is spiritual aliveness.

In sanctification there is yieldedness to God: "Yield yourselves unto God." Yieldedness is based on the principle of identification. Parents identify with the joys and hurts of their children. We identify with a new acquaintance because he is a friend of our old friend, and anyone who is his friend is our friend. At a much deeper level the Christian identifies with Christ. The Christian looks at the Cross and declares, "He did it for me. I belonged there, but He took my place." And the Christian looks at the risen Christ and identifies with His resurrection, affirming, "There I am also." Christ was tempted before His death but not after it. After the Resurrection Christ was beyond the gravitational pull of sin. He was in heaven's orbit. In a lesser way the Christian (1) who has died to sin and is alive in Christ (2) is identified completely with Him in a life fully yielded to His service. He is in the world but not of it.

In sanctification there is freedom from sin: "Sin shall not have dominion over you" (Rom. 6:14). It is a strange fact that some Christians believe God has the power to forgive sins committed against Him, but not the power to cleanse sin from the heart. This limits our Lord's saving power and denies His sovereignty.

In sanctification there is fulfillment: "Ye have your fruit unto holiness." Christians are not sanctified to live life in a special ghetto, far removed from the real world. But the attitudes, emotions, and will are cleansed of the sin nature. This sanctification is wrought by the Holy Spirit in the believer, so that we may truly reflect a Christian set of attitudes, a Christian way of feeling about ourselves and others, and a Christian way of conducting ourselves. This Christian character is not legalistic, for it cannot be legislated. This kind of life-style comes by the indwelling presence of the Holy Spirit as described by Paul in Galatians: "But the fruit of the Spirit is love, joy, peace, longsuffering, gentleness, goodness, faith, meekness, temperance: against such there is no law" (Gal. 5:22-23). This is truly the fulfilled life.

Chapter 23

Life in the Spirit

The eighth chapter of Romans is an important mountain peak in the theology of Paul, as well as a high spiritual vista in the high plateau of the New Testament. More clearly than any other New Testament passage, this chapter tells the things that are paramount for the Christian enjoying his new life in the Spirit. There are at least five benefits provided for the Spirit-filled Christian.

Freedom from Failure

A Scriptural Stepping-stone . . .

There is therefore now *no condemnation* to them which are in Christ Jesus, who walk not after the flesh, but after the Spirit. For the law of the *Spirit of life* in Christ Jesus hath made me *free from the law of sin and death.*

Rom. 8:1-2

* * *

Paul had a natural appreciation for rules and regulations. He was a man of the Sanhedrin who had, through his early adult years, checked himself systematically on all of their 613 rules. But keeping rules never gave him a free spirit. Under the law he had found his will was too weak to cope. He said, "For what I would, that do I not; but what I hate, that do I" (Rom. 7:15). He suffered from terrible feelings of guilt: "When I would do good, evil is present with me" (v. 21). And he further suffered from deep feelings of inadequacy, crying out, "O wretched man that I am!" (v. 24). But in Christ Jesus he was now set free. A new law now dominated his life, which was "the law of the Spirit of life in Christ Jesus" (8:2). He was no longer hidebound and restricted by a worrisome, detailed law that dominated him like a shrew. He was now set free in the fullness of Christ to keep the spirit of the law, not from fear of failure, but in loving respect; not in inadequacy and guilt, but in power and victory.

Freedom from Fear

A Scriptural Stepping-stone . . .

For *as many as are led by the Spirit* of God, they *are the sons of God.* For ye *have not received the spirit of bondage again to fear;* but ye have received the *Spirit of adoption,* whereby we cry, Abba, Father.

Rom. 8:14-15

*   *   *

The Spirit-filled Christian is set free from fear, just as a child has no fear of his loving father.

It is wonderful to feel the job you are in is the result of all your lifetime preparation and experiences up until now. It is great to feel your home is a happier and better place to live than it was 5 or 10 years ago. It is wonderful to feel your life is an open book with exciting and marvelous things yet un-known out over the horizons and around the bends of the road ahead. This is the very opposite of an existence that is lived under condemnation, groveling in guilt, wallowing in feelings of inadequacy, with a sense of futility and frustration. The word "Abba" used in the King James Version actually means "Daddy" in the original language. This indicates the Spirit-filled person is in a relationship with God that makes His presence intimate and real through every kind of circum-stance. To the Spirit-led person, God is always close at hand and thoroughly approachable. There is an inner confidence that helps us know He cares.

Help in Our Prayers

A Scriptural Stepping-stone . . .

> Likewise the *Spirit also helpeth our infirmities:* for we know not what we should pray for as we ought: but the *Spirit itself maketh intercession for us* with groanings which cannot be uttered.
>
> Rom. 8:26

*   *   *

The Holy Spirit strengthens and deepens a Christian's prayer life. Who is there who knows exactly how to pray? Do we pray for our children never to get hurt or never to have problems and difficulties? Tough experiences are often the making of people. And no one is ever mature who has not gone through difficult places, where he was thrown back fully on resources beyond himself. Do we pray for God to give us a

161

new job? A new job might be bad. A pot of gold may be the last thing on earth we need. Knowing how to pray is no easy matter. But for the Spirit-filled person there is an inner Presence making intercession with thoughts we may not be able to articulate. When you don't know how to pray, let the Spirit do your praying for you.

Perspectives on Hard Times

A Scriptural Stepping-stone . . .

And we know that *all things work together for good* to them that love God, to them who are the called *according to his purpose.*

Rom. 8:28

*　　*　　*

The Holy Spirit takes everything that happens to us and makes it work out for good. No one is going to say that everything that happens to us is precisely God's will. People interfere with God's will and become second causes in things that hurt us. There are accidents in life that are the results of freedom in the universe. If we enjoy the blessings of freedom, we also must accept its liabilities. The rain and the tornado bring their blessings and their destruction to both the righteous and the unrighteous. But the fact is that God will take whatever experiences come into our lives and will cause the worse kind of problem to work out for some good in our lives and for His glory.

A Scriptural Stepping-stone . . .

> For *I am persuaded, that neither death, nor life,* nor
> angels, nor principalities, nor powers, nor things
> present, nor things to come, nor height, nor depth,
> nor any other creature, *shall be able to separate us*
> *from the love of God,* which is in Christ Jesus our
> Lord.
>
> Rom. 8:38-39

*　　*　　*

The fullness of the Holy Spirit gives the assurance of eternal life in Christ. There is no circumstance with which the Spirit-filled Christian cannot cope. Paul was persuaded that nothing could separate him from the love of God, which is in Christ Jesus our Lord.

This confidence in Christ is not the glib eternal security that says that once I believe in Christ, there is nothing I can ever do that will cause me to be lost. True faith is the deep, abiding security of the Spirit-filled Christian whose continuing commitment to Jesus Christ assures him of God's blessings in this life and the life to come.

If your home is a hard place to live, the Holy Spirit has the strength you need to be a victor instead of a victim. Are you frustrated in making decisions concerning the future for yourself and your family? The Holy Spirit has the clearness of mind that will help you understand His leadings. Are you confused about how you should pray for yourself and your loved ones? Let the Holy Spirit teach you what His intercession means for you. Are you serving God primarily out of fear? Let the Holy Spirit set you free from the bondage of sin and death by the power of the Spirit for a fulfilled life in Christ Jesus.

Chapter 24

Sin and the Sanctified Life

Paul's letter to the Romans follows a logical sequence: (1) Paul uses most of the first three chapters (1:18—3:20) discussing the frightening problem of God's wrath and man's sin. (2) Then he talks about justification by faith (3:21—4:25). (3) And in natural sequence following his exploration of justification, Paul discusses sanctification and life in the Spirit (5—8).

Shall We Sin?

A Scriptural Stepping-stone . . .

There can be no life in the Spirit unless there is freedom from sin: "What shall we say then? Shall we continue in sin, that grace may abound? God forbid. *How shall we, that are dead to sin, live any longer therein?* . . . Knowing this, that our old man is crucified with him, *that the body of sin might be destroyed,* that henceforth we should not serve sin. . . . Likewise *reckon ye also yourselves to be dead indeed unto sin,* but alive unto God through Jesus Christ our Lord" (Rom. 6:1-2, 6, 11).

*　*　*

The Book of Romans ending with chapter 4 is like an Easter week ending on Saturday, or the Christmas season ending on December 24. Justification by faith leads to sanctification by faith. Paul makes it plain that justification is not just a courtroom term that describes a way of changing the legal light on a person without changing his nature. It is not justification on a technicality of the law. Forgiveness is accompanied by freedom from the sinful nature and worldly lifestyle through sanctification.

Can Sin Be Destroyed?

Freedom from sin is knowable in the same way crucifixion and death are knowable: *"Knowing this,* that our old man is crucified with him, that the body of sin might be destroyed, that henceforth we should not serve sin"* (Rom. 6:6).

There are three ways the gospel may be misunderstood. (1) Lack of instruction may result in Christians who believe but do not understand the gospel they believe. This is why Peter, a contemporary colleague in the gospel with Paul, urged believers to be able to give a reason for the hope within them (1 Pet. 3:15). Then (2) the gospel may be misunderstood because persons are dull of learning. There are good citizens who love their country and will fight for it who do not know or understand the Constitution. One of the claims of the gospel is that faith, not knowledge, is the way to salvation. Not everyone has the gift of learning. Since most people are ordinary learners, it is good that brilliance is not necessary for salvation. (3) Others misunderstand the gospel because they choose to distort the gospel for their own purposes through deviousness.

In this instance, Paul was thinking about actual people whom he knew, probably in Corinth, who had tried to distort the gospel by asking him if they should not keep on indulging in sins of the flesh so the grace of forgiveness could abound all the more. Paul's first response was a firm "God forbid."

Grace and Sin

In this paragraph (Rom. 6:4-11) Paul uses a series of statements and phrases to describe how grace overcomes sin. First, "We are *buried with him by baptism*" (v. 4). The water in a baptismal tank and the pastor's act of submerging the believer beneath it does not cleanse the heart of sin. But baptism is an excellent symbol of faith in action. As the believer closes his eyes, takes a deep breath, and sinks into the pool until he feels the water closing in over his head, it is as though he were being buried with Christ. His old self-centeredness is gone, buried, departed; he rises to testify that Christ is the Lord of his life.

Second, we also should *"walk in newness of life"* (Rom. 6:4). There is no way to be raised up from burial with Christ without living a resurrected life. We are not resurrected to old sins and defeating habits of life, but to a whole new life of joy in the Spirit.

Third, *"Our old man is crucified* with him, that the body of sin might be destroyed" (Rom. 6:6). There is no need for the Christian to serve sin anymore, because the person who once lived is now crucified, dead, and buried, and the body of sin is destroyed.

Fourth, *"He that is dead is freed from sin"* (Rom. 6:7). How can there be a more clear statement on freedom from sin? God forbid that we should sell short the power of the gospel to set men and women free from sin. God forbid that we should limit the power of Christ to forgiveness, and not include cleansing.

Fifth, "Likewise *reckon . . . yourselves to be dead indeed unto sin,* but alive unto God" (Rom. 6:11). There are no lifeless Christians, only Christians who are alive through the resurrection of Christ our Lord. There is no theology that teaches there will be any sin in heaven. But there is some difference among us on when sin is eliminated. (1) Some believe sin is forgiven and cleansed, all at the same time, in the new birth. This is like believing in being born and baptized in the same moment. (2) Some believe sin is cleansed at the moment of death. (3) Our Roman Catholic friends believe sin is cleansed in purgatory following death. (4) Still others believe sin is eliminated a little at a time with sanctification only as process. (5) But Paul believed that cleansing was the instantaneous work of the Holy Spirit in believers' hearts after they were born again, in the here and now.

Chapter 25

The Agony of
Lost Loved Ones

In a recent conference, the speaker asked everyone to come forward to pray who had a concern for unconverted family members. A great proportion of that large audience responded, many weeping, and all of them with expressions of spiritual concern on their faces. I was amazed at the proportion of the audience who were obviously intense enough about the salvation of their loved ones to go to their knees publicly.

What do Christians do when the friends and family who are closest to them do not believe and accept Christ as Lord of their lives? There are at least three options: (1) Christians with lost loved ones can despair. It is easy enough to blame people and circumstances for the resistance our children or other loved ones have against the gospel. The handwringing Christian usually begins his explanations on lost loved ones by shifting blame on others. It is the fault of a stern father, an insensitive pastor, or a church blowup. (2) Christians with lost loved ones can wait for others to win them. It takes no faith to do nothing. Callous unconcern is little worse than concern without action. It doesn't take much effort to be a friend, even to someone in one's own family. (3) Christians with lost loved ones can become involved in their salvation. It takes faith, hope, and love to demonstrate acceptance of unsaved loved ones when our concern for their salvation is spurned. Genuine, unmanipulative friendship is hard to beat when it comes to forging a relationship from which a desire is kindled for Christ.

There is a dimension of irony in our ministry when any of us who are effective in winning and serving others cannot reach our own "kinsmen" (Rom. 9:3), as Paul calls them. Some of the most hurt people I know are ministers and lay leaders who are unable to lead their own families to know and love Christ. Paul was the first and foremost spokesman of the church to the Gentiles, all the while he, as a Jew, longed to bring his own people to love the Lord. Winning Gentiles was his second choice after he was rejected by his own people.

The favored-nation status of the Jews was similar in many ways to the favored relationship of unsaved children in parsonages and Christian laymen's homes: (1) *Paul's kinsmen had every reason to accept Christ because of the many blessings God had brought to them.* In a unique way, they were chosen people. Like many of our families, they were people with special privileges and blessings. (2) *Paul's kinsmen had seen the glory of God.* The Shekinah was the divine splendor of light that descended when God was visiting His people (see Exod. 16:10; 24:16-17; 29:43). But in spite of the glory they had witnessed, Israel had rejected Christ. (3) *Paul's kinsmen had received the covenants of God:* These were covenants *(a)* in the promise of the rainbow after the Flood; *(b)* in the promise of blessing to Abraham, their first patriarch and hero; *(c)* in the law at Mount Sinai; and *(d)* in the new promise of God in the Redeemer, Christ Jesus. (4) *Paul's kinsmen had the law of God.* They were respectable citizens and decent people. They revered the law and followed it meticulously in daily living.

(5) *Paul's kinsmen had a great religious heritage* including the great Temple in Jerusalem. Their failure to believe in Christ is the heartache and burden Paul shares with many Christians in families today.

There are four ideas that cast light on the relationships Christians may maintain with their unsaved loved ones:

First, Paul settled on a minimum faith that would bring his loved ones to Christ. It is interesting that in the three agonizing chapters about his kinsmen, Roman 9—11, Paul does not once say or suggest they had to believe or even agree with all he wrote, to be saved. But he did give an irreducible minimum as a beginner's creed for salvation. (1) The believer accepts Christ as Lord. (2) The believer accepts the resurrection of Jesus as fact. (3) A believer not only accepts the Lordship of Christ with his heart but also confesses his faith with his lips. "For with *the heart* man believeth unto righteousness; and with *the mouth* confession is made unto salvation" (Rom. 10:10).

Second, Paul found hope in the whosoever of faith: "For *whosoever* shall call upon the name of the Lord shall be saved" (Rom. 10:13).

This promise is a double blessing, for it includes everyone, and it does not exclude anyone. There is still hope for your loved ones because the God who loves them is only waiting for their call.

Third is a need for the actual hearing of the Good News: "How then shall they call on him in whom they have not believed? and how shall they believe in him of whom they have not *heard?* and how shall they *hear* without a preacher?

And how shall they preach, except they be sent? as it is written, How beautiful are the feet of them that preach the gospel of peace, and bring *glad tidings* of good things!" (Rom. 10:14-15).

These words have traditionally been great missionary texts for evangelism in faraway places. But Paul was talking about his kinsmen who were near at hand, right in his own country and in his own home. Turned-off Christians find it hard to tune in on the Good News that they have distorted and garbled for so long. They have hearing without understanding. They hear the sound of the gospel without ever catching its ring of truth.

Fourth is the right of rejection: "I was made manifest unto *them that asked not after me.* . . . All day long I have stretched forth my hands unto a disobedient and gainsaying people" (Rom. 10:20-21). Even after the most fervent prayers and heaviest of burdens there are people who do not see, hear, feel, or savor the gospel.

When does a Christian stop praying for the salvation of non-Christians in the family? Never! But there comes a time when continuing a burden at the level of concern that affects emotional and even physical health is not to the glory of God. It may take more faith to commit a son or daughter into God's hands than it does to keep up a self-defeating, joy-reducing, self-destructing cycle of concern that tends to omit or downgrade the many blessings of God and to forget whatever prayers have been answered. There comes a time when each of our lost loved ones must be committed into the hands of God.

Chapter 26

Never Give Up

A Scriptural Stepping-stone . . .

What shall we say then? Is there unrighteousness with God? God forbid. For he saith to Moses, I will have mercy on whom I will have mercy, and I will have compassion on whom I will have compassion. So then it is not of him that willeth, nor of him that runneth, but of God that sheweth mercy. For the scripture saith unto Pharaoh, Even for this same purpose have I raised thee up, that I might shew my power in thee, and that my name might be declared throughout all the earth. Therefore hath he mercy on whom he will have mercy, and whom he will he hardeneth.

Rom. 9:14-18

* * *

The questions concerning unsaved family that tormented Paul's mind are the same ones that haunt the minds of 20th-century Christians who are burdened for their loved ones. (1) Has God failed to reach the Jews? (2) Has God withdrawn himself and cast them off? (3) What is wrong with the Jews who seem to be hardened? (4) Are they going to be finally and ultimately lost?

The Jews were more than unresponsive; they had become hostile. Paul himself had been ordered out of their synagogues. They had slandered him; they browbeat his converts, making their Christian witness difficult if not impossible. They had beat him and plotted against his life; and, as Paul must certainly have known, the end of his troubles with unconverted Jews was nowhere in sight.

But in spite of all the problems the Jews made for him, he still loved his own people and races: *"My heart's desire and prayer to God* for Israel is, that they might be saved"* (Rom. 10:1). Paul's struggle is like a mirror image of the difficulties many Christians have in living with themselves when their loved ones are lost.

Paul's earnestness in seeking a reason for the lost people of his family caused him to ask a foolish question: Has God failed us? "Is there unrighteousness with God?" Paul's fast, firm answer to the thought that God has failed his loved ones is "God forbid" (Rom. 9:14). The sovereignty of God does not mean He arbitrarily saves whom He will save and damns whom he will damn. Paul uses two illustrations to make his point on why some men respond in faith and fellowship with God while others' hearts are hardened.

On Sinai, following Moses' great prayer of intercession for his people, Moses needed new assurance and a new vision for his work. He prayed, "I beseech thee, shew me thy glory." And God replied, "I will make all my goodness pass before thee, and I will . . . be *gracious to whom I will be gracious"* (Exod. 33:19). Some think this means God chooses arbitrarily and capriciously to extend mercy to some, while others of equal faith and commitment to God may receive His wrath and not His mercy and compassion. No! Mercy and compassion are intended for all who seek His face.

Paul's other reference is to the hardening of the spiritual arteries in Pharaoh's heart. "For this cause have *I raised thee up, for to shew in thee my power;* ... As yet exaltest thou thyself against my people, that thou wilt not let them go?" (Exod. 9:16-17; Rom. 9:16-17). Some believe God raised up a puppet king for the purpose of hardening his heart and giving God a chance to prove His power. I don't think so. I believe the facts of history would have been altered if Pharaoh had sought and followed the will of God in his life. But when he did not, his heart became hard and he suffered the consequences, just like anyone else who persists in going against the will of God in his life.

There are three ways to look at how the facts of history have come to nations, races of people, or in persons' individual lives: (1) History is an impersonal force, the product of a process beyond the control of anyone. (2) History is chance, a record of how events happened to work out. Or, (3) History is the revelation of God's purposes, the working of a divine will moving in harmony with moral purposes.

In a sense, all three of these factors—impersonal force, chance, and purpose—function in history, the divine will dominating the other two. There are forces beyond our control and chance factors that can scarcely be ignored. But there has always been the ever-moving presence of the divine will, calling, guiding, and directing the affairs of men.

Second, God's people have always been a minority in the world: "A remnant" shall be saved (Rom. 11:5). It has always been so. (1) Abraham left his home near the Persian Gulf to emigrate as a minority family to a place God had not yet named when he and his people sold out and hit the road. No other families in the area shared his faith. (2) The Hebrews were a minority in Egypt, eventually reduced to slaves in work camps. (3) Believers were certainly a minority at Golgotha. (4) Christians were a minority throughout the Roman Empire in Paul's day. (5) True Christians are a small minority in the world today. (6) And in your community, it is more likely than not that you are part of a Christian minority even though it is claimed there are 40 million evangelical Christians in the United States alone.

Third, there is always hope for our loved ones to be saved: "And so all Israel shall be saved" (Rom. 11:26). At the close of his long struggle over the lostness of his kinsmen, Paul ended on a note of hope. God had not yet saved them, but there was still hope. God's mercy is not withdrawn. "For God hath concluded them all in unbelief, that he might have mercy upon all" (v. 32). We can live with ourselves as long as we keep hope alive.

Few problems faced by Christian families are more vexing than what to do about unsaved members of the family. Several things need to be avoided: (1) Nagging and pleading turns off most people. (2) Preaching at people and pointing out their failures only drives them farther away from God and the church. (3) Ignoring their lostness is not consistent with Christian love and compassion. (4) Manipulating circumstances often backfires. (5) But the one thing we can do is live a gracious Christian life before them while we never give up hope.

Chapter 27

A New Way to Live

A thousand miles from Jerusalem, in the family area of a hillside house in Rome, a group of Christians were gathered to hear read aloud the final portion of a letter from a prospective visitor named Paul.

They listened incredulously as he described his own personal heartache over the Jews who had galvanized their minds against Christ with impenetrable walls of rejection and hostility (Rom. 9:11). They must have been moved when he wrote, "I have great heaviness and continual sorrow in my heart" over their attitudes (v. 2). But they must have been startled when they heard the reader quote Paul, "I could wish that myself were accursed from Christ for my brethren, my kinsmen" (v. 3). Then came a pause with time for the reader to clear his throat, and finally the word of encouragement from Paul that all the family could be saved: "For God hath concluded them all in unbelief, that he might have mercy upon all" (11:32).

The group might have expected Paul to end with his searching discussion of how the chosen people could be actually lost when they had enjoyed a favored-nation status with God (Rom. 10:11). Instead, there was a pause and then an assurance that the people of the promise could receive the promise and not be lost.

Then with a ringing "therefore" (Rom. 12:1), which must have ricocheted off the hard surfaces of plastered walls and marble floor, the reader of Paul's letter to the Roman Christians began the section on how justification and sanctification apply to daily experiences. The Good News about God and His mercy that sets the person free from a self-made prison is not some intriguing idea to think about. If all we do is listen to the Good News, we have not really heard. But if we hear and believe, there follows inevitably the "therefore" of a new way to live.

This is a good place to stop for an explanation of the difference between justification and sanctification. Justification is forgiveness for sins committed, while sanctification is the cleansing of sin's pollution and power. Justification takes away sins, while sanctification takes away sin. Justification deals with the status of man as a sinner, while sanctification deals with the state of man's nature. Justification is accompanied by repentance and faith, while a man is sanctified entirely when God has all of him there is, when he becomes a living sacrifice.

There is a sense in which justification and sanctification stand apart, while at the same time they merge. Sanctification is no take-it-or-leave-it extra, it is welded to justification. Sanctification is an integral part of salvation. No Christian can accept justification and ignore sanctification, and no Christian can be wholly sanctified apart from the grace of forgiveness and regeneration.

The idea of sacrifice was not new to the Jewish audience who heard Paul's letter. But the idea of a living sacrifice was both startling and new. Several ideas are included in Paul's call for living sacrifices that also apply to us as they did to those first-generation Christians in Rome.

∗   ∗   ∗

A Scriptural Stepping-stone . . .

> I beseech you therefore, brethren, by the mercies of God, that ye *present your bodies* a living sacrifice, holy, acceptable unto God, which is your reasonable service. And *be not conformed* to this world: but *be ye transformed* by the renewing of your mind, that ye may prove what is that good, and acceptable, and *perfect, will of God.*

Rom. 12:1-2

For the Love of Mercy

A Christian does not sacrifice himself to earn God's favor but to respond to His mercy. We are "brethren, by the mercies of God" (Rom. 12:1). Paul did not throw out good works in the early segments of his discussion on salvation to bring them back through the side door in words about a transformed life. No man can earn God's mercy by good works. But no man who has received God's mercies in justification can withhold the sacrifice of himself to God in gratitude. The fountains of his motivations are cleansed of self-serving and self-righteousness to allow the heart of thanksgiving to flow freely.

The Importance of Your Body

The inner self cannot be separated from the body. That is why Paul urged, "Present your bodies a living sacrifice"

179

(Rom. 12:1). (1) This is why the body must be properly maintained. It never functions well when overstressed, ignored, or fatigued. (2) This is why personal habits need to work with the body and not against it. (3) This is why every Christian has to come to terms with his body, whether it is old, young, strong, frail, beautiful, or ugly.

Some Christians develop non-Christian attitudes and behave in self-defeating ways because they cannot accept the height, the age, or the color of their body. Some people have gone through life creating problems for their Christian witness just because they couldn't accept the fact they were short of stature. There is no way a Christian can present his spirit to God and ignore his body.

Service and Sacrifice

Christians are not holy persons set apart as objects for adoration. They are "a living sacrifice . . . which is your reasonable service" (Rom. 12:1). Some Christians are trying to be like guilded lilies while people get the feeling they would turn brown or bruise if somebody touched them. Is it more holy to sit in a retreat house and say prayers or to serve rice to the maimed and diseased pavement people in Bombay? Sanctification as the completion of the work that God does in regeneration is for the purpose of service.

An Alternate Life-style

Paul directed, "Be not conformed to this world" (Rom. 12:2). Another translator has said, "Don't copy the behavior and customs of this world" (TLB). In the state of Maine where we had a place in an oceanside village, I had difficulty explaining my Christian standards to a neighbor who seemingly had no concept of evangelical Christianity. One day he told me about his daughter, a Vassar graduate who had chosen an alternate life-style by moving to a commune near Santa Fe, N.Mex. I hit on his idea of an alternate life-style to explain our Christian standards. Then I explained to him that our family had done something like that, for we had broken out from the usually accepted secular ways of the culture and had chosen an alternate life-style. Since the days of the Roman Empire, Christians have gone against the mainstream as a cultural minority who had chosen a different way to live.

The Transformed Mind

Some Christians seem to feel they are transformed by their emotions. Therefore they go to churches that major on emotional services and emotional experiences. Others depend on rigid commitments to inflexible systems of rules and regulations. These kinds of people are forever coming out from congregations who disagree with them to seek a more hospitable fellowship or to start a new one. Still others depend on the authority of the church for their religious certainty. But only a change in the mind can change the whole personality. That is why Paul ordered, "Be ye transformed by the renewing of your mind" (Rom. 12:2).

The Perfect Will of God

Paul concluded that the transformed mind was the royal road to a transformed life: "That ye may prove . . . [the] perfect will of God" (Rom. 12:2). There is a matching word in another of Paul's letters that fits in tandem with this idea: "For this is the will of God, even your sanctification" (1 Thess. 4:3). The Christian whose life is a living sacrifice to God will always be sensitive to the will of God in every decision of life. The transformed mind, which leads us directly to the dominion and will of God in our lives, is the most direct route to a fulfilled life.

Chapter 28

On Getting Along with Each Other

A Scriptural Stepping-stone . . .

> Let every soul be subject unto the higher powers. For there is no power but of God: the powers that be are ordained of God. Whosoever therefore resisteth the power, resisteth the ordinance of God: and they that resist shall receive to themselves damnation. . . . Wherefore ye must needs be subject, not only for wrath, but also for conscience sake.
>
> Rom. 13:1-2, 5

*   *   *

There are several reasons why getting along with people in the church is often complicated. First, Christians have a high level of expectation for each other. Because people are in the church we expect them to keep their cool, always rejoice in everybody else's successes, never feel uncomfortable when they are put on the spot, respond to pressures with smiles and amens, close their eyes to contradictions and hypocrisies, and in general never fail to fulfill the role of the perfect church-man. But for good or ill, life doesn't work like that, even in the church. People are people and we almost never fulfill all of each other's expectations.

Second, Christians tend to impose their private notions on their circle of influence within the congregation. This means that many ideas that have more cultural roots than biblical foundations are considered as moral judgment and passed on with a stamp of religious authority. This creates a tendency for strong personalities to dominate weaker ones and for the strong to clash with each other.

Third, people within a congregation are often involved with each other at many levels besides church attendance. But whether people are in the church or outside the church, the problems of human relations tend to be quite similar. Besides cultural, ethnic, and subcultural clashes in values and priorities, there are some general personality problems that are commonly faced by people who are concerned with people.

Deviousness

First, deviousness often becomes a lifelong behavioral pattern with those who practice it. The writer of Proverbs had some pointed things to say about people who act like a friend for private reasons: "Bread of deceit is sweet to a man; but afterwards his mouth shall be filled with gravel" (20:17). "As a mad man who casteth firebrands, arrows, and death, so is the man that deceiveth his neighbour, and saith, Am not I in sport?" (26:18-19).

The credibility gap can create more tensions than most people can absorb. Promoting ideas and programs outwardly for the good of everyone when they are primarily for private purposes will sooner or later be found out. Telling part of the truth while withholding vital factors that would simplify the truth destroys confidence. When faith and confidence have been tarnished by irresponsibility, the original feeling of trust is hard to regain, if ever.

The exploitive approach to interpersonal relationships usually demonstrates itself in the efforts of one person to manipulate people and situations to his own advantage. In extreme form, this leads to outright lying and stealing. But more often manipulation results in making all transactions in the relationship tend to favor one person.

Rebellion

Second, people who continue their teenage rebellion into adulthood are hard to get along with. A man 40 years old who behaves toward his wife like he did toward his mother when he was 15 is still fighting the battles of adolescence. It is the nature of teenagers to rebel. Rebellion, within limits, is part of the process of cutting the apron strings. But an adult who continues to rebel against all authority figures is a very unhappy, disconsolate person.

Hostility

Third, it is difficult to have good human relations with any person who is basically hostile. A hostile person has a tendency, usually when associated with authority, to be antagonistic and suspicious toward other people. When hostility is openly expressed, it creates immediate problems in a relationship. But when hostility is suppressed, it has an equally disruptive quality that results in persons becoming gossipy and overly competitive.

Anger in a hostile person always lurks just below the surface. It is so generalized toward life that almost anything will provoke its outburst. If you are forced to deal with hostile people, try to avoid angry outbursts by keeping personal encounters shallow and at a minimum.

Inadequacy

Fourth, people with inferiority feelings always tend to be defensive in their relationships. Every human being under certain circumstances has feelings of inadequacy and inferiority. However, the person whose relationships are dominated by these feelings has a basic lack of self-confidence and self-esteem. The result is an oversensitiveness to threat or an exaggerated effort to prove one's own adequacy and worth by such techniques as boasting and showing off. Feelings of inferiority also tend to make one hypercritical of other people. Such people are especially difficult to deal with and may leave one feeling like the effort to communicate is not worth it.

Cynicism

Finally, the cynical person whose life is void of God's Spirit often lives in emotional insulation on purpose. Among the saddest cases of emotional insulation are people who were once deeply involved with a pastor and congregation they loved, but through unfortunate developments have suffered emotional hurt. Many of these make up their minds never to get emotionally involved in the church again, firmly insulating themselves from the joy and fulfillment that a good church relationship can bring.

But there is a cure for people who are inept in personal relations: (1) Accept yourself for what you are. (2) Find some person who will be nonjudgmental in discussing these problems with you openly and in stark frankness. (3) As much as possible trace back these unproductive attitudes and patterns to their childhood sources. (4) Come to God for forgiveness and cleansing (1 John 1:9).

Chapter 29

Questionable Things and Places

Mark Twain once said, "I am not bothered by what I do not understand about the Bible, but by what I do." In a *Herald of Holiness* article, May 7, 1952, Dr. G. B. Williamson spoke to the gray area of Christian behavior, where decisions are many times difficult to make, by appealing to an enlightened conscience. He said, "Uncivilized people in their darkness and superstition have sought to guard themselves by a taboo system. The Christian method has been to enlighten the conscience by the knowledge of moral standards, according . . . to God's Word."

A significant passage in the writings of Paul, which deals with questionable things and places, is the 14th chapter of Romans. Paul makes seven observations on questionable things and places that are as useful now in a highly technical society as they were in the days of slavery and gladiatorial combats.

*   *   *

A Scriptural Stepping-stone . . .

Paul's first admonition is to stay clear of making issues out of minor problems: *"Him that is weak in the faith receive ye, but not to doubtful dis-*

putations. For one believeth that he may eat all things: another, who is weak, eateth herbs. Let not him that eateth despise him that eateth not; and let not him which eateth not judge him that eateth: for God hath received him" (Rom. 14:1-3).

* * *

Paul opened his discussion on the law of love concerning doubtful things by warning against debates on matters of dietary rules and regulations which are of minor concern and often a private matter.

* * *

A Scriptural Stepping-stone . . .

Paul's second admonition is to be hard in judging yourself but always easy in your judgments on others. *"Who art thou that judgest another man's servant? to his own master he standeth or falleth. Yea, he shall be holden up: for God is able to make him stand. One man esteemeth one day above another:* another esteemeth every day alike. Let every man *be fully persuaded* in his own mind" (Rom. 14:4-5).

* * *

One of the troubling concerns among new Christians in the ancient world were the days on which they would pray and fast. Some chose one day and others another, while still others believed the day of the week did not matter. Some wanted to fast on the day Jesus was crucified, Friday. Others thought it better to fast on Saturday, which was the day the tomb stayed sealed. Still more wanted a day of self-discipline during a regular working schedule in the middle of the week. Paul's solution seemed to be that every man should be fully persuaded in his own mind and then be very slow in judging others. And in whatever decision is made, a prayer of thanks should be given to God as an act of worship, and not taken as an opportunity for calling down judgment on the heads of those who disagree.

*   *   *

A Scriptural Stepping-stone ...

Paul's third admonition was to make decisions in the gray areas of Christian ethics with an eye for protecting the weaker Christians. "For *none of us liveth to himself,* and no man dieth to himself. ... But why dost thou judge thy brother? or why dost thou set at nought thy brother? for we shall all stand before the judgment seat of Christ. ... *Let us not therefore judge one another any more:* but judge this rather, that *no man put a stumblingblock* or an occasion to fall in his brother's way" (Rom. 14:7, 10, 13).

*   *   *

One of the easiest things for older Christians to do is accept their own standards of behavior and ethics as the norm for everyone. Many a father has alienated his teenage son by trying to enforce harshly his own ideas on him. Paul's solution to the matter of differing opinions in matters not covered specifically in Scripture is to make one's own decisions and behave with an understanding of what is responsible or irresponsible in the sight of God.

*   *   *

A Scriptural Stepping-stone . . .

Paul's fourth admonition was to be careful lest their insistence on personal freedom destroy a much-needed influence for Christ. "I know, and am persuaded by the Lord Jesus, that *there is nothing unclean of itself:* but to him that esteemeth any thing to be unclean, to him it is unclean. But if thy brother be grieved with thy meat, now walkest thou not charitably. *Destroy not him with thy meat,* for whom Christ died. Let not then your good be evil spoken of" (Rom. 14:14-16).

*   *   *

In our eagerness to lead a separated life that is fully committed to Christ, a Christian can become involved in attitudes and behavior that put his entire witness in suspicion. It may be better for a Christian to accept the group conscience or the corporate conscience of the church when it does not necessarily comply with his own inner values, just for the sake of his continuing influence for Jesus Christ. "Let not then your good be evil spoken of" (Rom. 14:16).

There is nothing evil in a long strip of celluloid with emulsion on one side, which has been developed into a negative film that produces a picture that seems to move. This film process may be used for good in transmission of the gospel, medical histories of surgery, and missionary messages; or it may be put to pornographic use in the hands of men whose minds are depraved and whose purposes are motivated by greed. It is not the film process that is good or evil, but the persons who use it.

*   *   *

A Scriptural Stepping-stone . . .

Paul's fifth admonition was a reminder that the kingdom of God is bigger than rules. "For *the kingdom of God* is *not meat* and drink; *but righteousness, and peace, and joy* in the Holy Ghost. . . . Let us therefore follow after the things which make for peace, and things wherewith one may edify another" (Rom. 14:17, 19).

*   *   *

Since the kingdom of God is more than rules on meat and drink, let us give attention to the more important matters of righteousness, peace, and joy in the Holy Ghost. For a group of Christians to be divided over rules and regulations is the work of the devil. The work of the Holy Spirit makes for peace that leads each person to edify and help the other.

*   *   *

A Scriptural Stepping-stone . . .

Paul's sixth admonition was a call for all Christians to guard their influence. "It is good neither to eat flesh, nor to drink wine, *nor any thing whereby thy brother stumbleth,* or is offended, or is made weak" (Rom. 14:21). If that verse of Scripture were applied to all of the doubtful decisions that must be made in the gray area of ethical living, many divisive matters would disappear in the church.

* * *

Paul's last admonition calls for honesty with ourselves. "Hast thou faith? have it to thyself before God. Happy is he that condemneth not himself in that thing which he alloweth. And he that doubteth is damned if he eat, because he eateth not of faith: for *whatsoever is not of faith is sin"* (Rom. 14:22-23).

It is an easy matter for young people driven by emotions and social pressure to rationalize many kinds of behavior in situations that are different from those their parents faced. But even when a good rationalization can be produced, this does not always mean that a Christian should go ahead in doubtful behavior against his own conscience. Where there is doubt, there is condemnation: "For whatsoever is not of faith is sin" (Rom. 14:23).

There are enough points of difference among us as people to divide every church, if the principles of the 14th chapter of Romans are ignored. But on the other hand, there is enough food for thought in this chapter to help guide Christians through the difficult decisions that must be made for themselves, and eventually for their own children, as they cope with the secular pressures of a world that lives with little regard for spiritual laws or the reality of God.

Chapter 30

A Christian and His Friends

It was not easy for Paul to close his letter to the Christians in Rome. He loved them and desired deeply to see them. He was writing from Corinth, but he told the Romans before he could come in person he needed first to go to Jerusalem. After Jerusalem he would come to Rome, and then on to Spain. Paul had a big dream that was cut short by Nero's persecution and eventual martyrdom. But time did not run out on Paul before he was able to go to Jerusalem to deliver a cash offering from the churches in Asia Minor.

There were many similarities between Paul's financial project for Jerusalem and the budget system for missions in the church today. In some ways, Paul's financial campaign for the headquarters church in Jerusalem was a prototype of centralized giving.

There was the need among Christians all around the Mediterranean world to keep the mother church alive. Christians in Jerusalem had lost their jobs from persecution and boycott. The Temple, which was the great employer in the area, was in outright opposition to the Christians. Many believers had left the area of Jerusalem for work in other world areas as far away as India on the one side and Rome on the other. These Christians in Rome would have fully understood the need of the Christians in Jerusalem.

Giving an offering to the congregation in Jerusalem helped demonstrate the unity of the Church across the world. Each congregation in the towns of modern Turkey and Greece was not an isolated, struggling congregation on its own. Each member belonged to a unified larger movement. Without doubt Paul would have understood and appreciated the denominational budget system today.

Giving to Jerusalem was love in action, a practical proof of stewardship. When ordinary people in the middle and lower classes gave an offering, they were giving a part of themselves. The farther down the economic scale a person lives, the more their offering must be a true representation of themselves. The two key words in giving are *love* and *stewardship*. The amount of the offering indicates the level of a person's stewardship, while the attitude of the giver identifies the degree of love the gift represents.

The Scripture never indicates that Paul's dream of going to Spain ever materialized. However, Paul's Philippian letter written from his cell not long before he was beheaded proves that his joy in the Holy Spirit and his confidence in the resurrected Christ never wavered even at the very end. Knowing about this turn of events, which Paul could not have foreseen, makes his closing remarks and greetings in the letter to Rome all the more inspiring.

There was a letter of commendation for a woman: "I commend unto you *Phebe our sister,* which is a servant of the church which is at Cenchrea" (Rom. 16:1).

Several observations can be made on this letter of commendation on a lady in the church. (1) Letters of instruction were common procedure in the ancient world. (2) It is the nature of Christians to extend help and hospitality to Christians from other congregations because of their common bond in Christ. (3) And, from the earliest days in the Church, there was significant work for women to do. It could be that Phebe was the courier who carried Paul's letter personally from Corinth to Rome. (4) There are no strangers in the family of Christ. Christian believers have always been a minority in the world. But they have always had a strong bond to each other.

Throughout his letter Paul did not talk down to the Roman Christians. His confidence in them and their faith came through in his opening paragraph (Rom. 1:8) and is sustained throughout. But in this last appeal he warns them against two kinds of troublemakers: (1) those who cause divisions, and (2) those who hinder and distort the faith of others.

* * *

A Scriptural Stepping-stone . . .

Brethren, *mark them which cause divisions . . .* and *avoid them.* For they that are such serve not our Lord Jesus Christ, but their own belly; and by good words and fair speeches *deceive the hearts of the simple. . . .* I would have you wise unto that which is good, and *simple concerning evil.*

Rom. 16:17-19

* * *

Paul further directed these Roman Christians in what to do with persons who sought to make trouble. (1) Identify troublemakers and do not allow their winsome ways to confuse you. The worst troublemakers in any church are the neurotics whose distorted perceptions of reality are peddled from person to person and church to church. Neurotics can be gifted and very attractive to a talent-hungry congregation. But given time, their real troublesome self comes through. (2) Avoid troublemakers as much as is possible. He does not say destroy them or even fight them, but stay out of their way. Don't give potential troublemakers places of responsibility unless you are ready to accept the consequences. (3) Learn to sort out and recognize the potential good in every person. Build on the useful qualities in a person and play down their flaws. (4) Be simplistic and naive in your fear of evil.

*　*　*

A Scriptural Stepping-stone ...

A man is known and judged by the kinds of friends he has. Paul mentions some of his who join him in his greetings to the Romans. *"Timotheus my workfellow,* and Lucius, and Jason, and Sosipater, *my kinsmen,* salute you. I *Tertius, who wrote* this epistle, salute you in the Lord. *Gaius mine host,* and of the whole church, saluteth you. *Erastus the chamberlain* of the city saluteth you, and *Quartus a brother"* (Rom. 16:21-23).

*　*　*

In one word or short phrase Paul characterizes each of his friends, including Tertius, the secretary who penned the letter; Gaius, his host; and others he referred to as fellow workers, kinsmen, and brothers.

Some principles we can derive from this include: (1) Friendships are built on associations. You can't be friends with someone you don't know. (2) Friendship is a two-way street. It is obvious that Paul and his friends were a part of each other. (3) Friends are an extension of ourselves. Our friends are a part of us. (4) The ultimate test of friendship is unconditional loyalty.

Paul closes his letter with a doxology. Paul had written about the awful sinfulness of man and his redemption through faith in Christ. He laid out the doctrine of entire sanctification. He took time to wrestle through the problem of his own kinsmen who rejected Christ. He wrote brilliantly of the ways Christian faith applies to the situations in life. And in his closing lines he admits his worries over going to Jerusalem. But, typically of Paul, he ends on a note of happy optimism with one of the great benedictions in the New Testament: "The grace of our Lord Jesus Christ be with you all. Amen. Now to him that is of power to stablish you according to my gospel, and the preaching of Jesus Christ, according to the revelation of the mystery, which was kept secret since the world began, but now is made manifest, and by the scriptures of the prophets, according to the commandment of the everlasting God, made known to all nations for the obedience of faith: to God only wise, be glory through Jesus Christ for ever. Amen" (Rom. 16:24-27).